CROSSING THE KEY STAGES OF HISTORY

Effective History Teaching
5–16 and Beyond

Edited by
Ruth Watts and Ian Grosvenor

David Fulton Publishers
London

David Fulton Publishers Ltd
2 Barbon Close, London WC1N 3JX

First published in Great Britain by
David Fulton Publishers 1995

Note: The right of Ruth Watts and Ian Grosvenor to be identified as the editors of this work has been asserted by them in accordance with the Copyright, Designs and Patents Act 1988.

Copyright © David Fulton Publishers Limited

British Library Cataloguing in Publication Data

A catalogue record for this book is available from the British Library

ISBN 1–85346–324–8

Typeset by Harrington & Co.
Printed in Great Britain by BPC Books and Journals, Exeter.

Contents

Acknowledgements

The editors thank Brenda Cox for her sterling work on preparing the final drafts of the manuscript for publication. They also thank Myra Dean and John Shearwood for computer assistance, Pru Morrison and Barry Williamson for their helpful comments on Chapter 2 and Sue Bennett and Ian Colwill, the history officers at SCAA, for answering their queries and involving them in consultation exercises on the revision of the National Curriculum in history.

Finally, the editors thank Sue Akehurst and Rob Watts for their patient help and advice throughout the writing and editing of this book.

Notes on Contributors

Sue Bardwell is Quality Learning Officer (History) for Staffordshire LEA and a registered OFSTED inspector. Previously she has worked as an LEA adviser in Sandwell and as an in-service trainer for history. She has taught across the 11–18 age range. In 1993–4 she was history teacher fellow at Newman College of Higher Education in Birmingham.

Paul Bracey is head of the history department in Park View Comprehensive School in Birmingham. He is a panel member of MEG and has been secretary of Midlands History Forum for several years. From 1991 to 1993 he was seconded to the University of Birmingham, School of Education to assist on the PGCE course.

Ian Grosvenor is Head of History at Newman College of Higher Education in Birmingham. He has taught in primary, secondary and special schools, led LEA anti-racist initiatives and worked in Equal Opportunities training. He has published articles on the teaching of history, post-1945 British education policy and is currently researching the educational experiences of refugees in Britain. He was recently awarded the George Cadbury Prize for his doctoral thesis by the University of Birmingham.

James Kilmartin is head of history at Bishop Walsh R.C. Comprehensive School in Sutton Coldfield. Previously he was head of history at St Phillip's R.C. Sixth Form College in Birmingham. He is a tutor for the Open University and has a doctorate in seventeenth century English history.

Chris Palmer is senior consultant for history in Birmingham Curriculum Support Service and an OFSTED inspector. He has taught history and English in primary and secondary schools. He has been a tutor on the GEST courses for history at the University of Birmingham, School of Education.

Erica Pounce is teacher consultant for history, Birmingham Curriculum Support Service. She has taught history in primary and secondary schools and ran Sandwell's Multicultural Resource Centre. She has researched and written articles on equal opportunities issues, citizenship, environmental education and cross-curricular themes. She has been a tutor on the GEST courses for history at the University of Birmingham, School of Education.

Peter Rogers is Senior Lecturer in History at Newman College of Higher Education in Birmingham. He has taught in East Africa, in secondary schools in the UK and was Director of the African and Asian Resources Centre at Newman College, 1979–90. He is a History Research Associate at the Centre for West African Studies, University of Birmingham. He currently teaches modern World history and pedagogy.

Ruth Watts is lecturer for education (history) at the University of Birmingham School of Education. She taught history in secondary schools for many years and has been secretary for the Standing Conference of History Teacher Educators in the UK since its inception. Her MA and doctorate were on the history of education, and she has written on this and on women's history and the teaching of history.

Introduction

In *Telling the Truth about History* (1994) Appleby, Hunt and Jacob cogently wrote that 'History':

> 'springs from the human fascination with self-discovery, from the persistent concern about the nature of existence and people's engagement with it. Men and women have learned to externalize this curiosity – even to distance themselves from its impertinent subjectivity – by directing their questions to concepts and abstractions...but the renewable source of energy behind these inquiries comes from an intense craving for information about what it is to be human'.

Their book eloquently advanced a very topical and persuasive argument for the pivotal role of history in a democratic society. In Britain in the 1980s and 1990s the position of history in schools has been a contested area. Although originally it became a foundation subject of the National Curriculum with pupils entitled to study it from 5 to 16, that entitlement was cut subsequently by 2 years, leaving history optional at GCSE level and thus appearing less important than those subjects which retained their full entitlement. This decision was encapped at the beginning of 1995 by the expedient but educationally unsound decision to make reporting on history in primary schools by OFSTED optional. Furthermore, the nature of what history should be studied was hotly debated, especially outside of the classroom. This, in itself, was perhaps actually illustrating the significance of such a political subject rather than the reverse. Anxiety that children should learn a 'correct' version of the past militated against desires to develop questioning attitudes in future citizens of a democratic society. Such contrary viewpoints led to widely differing arguments as to what should be in the history National Curriculum and how it should be taught.

The fact that 'everyone' **knew** what history should be taught demonstrated at least that it was widely considered that history did have an important role in forming the ideas of young people. The authors of this book certainly believe that history is a crucial humanities subject in a democratic society as well as being a fascinating and engaging one. After several years of constant change and evolution the National Curriculum for history 5 to 14 is set for 5 years, the new A/AS level core has been issued and the proposals for GCSE are drafted. It is now possible to take stock and ascertain what entitlement in history remains statutory for English and Welsh school pupils and what could be feasible over and above this. In this sense, it is intended to take up Nicholas Tate's (1994) challenge:

> 'The coming of a revised national curriculum marks the beginning of a new era. I hope it marks the beginning of a lively debate about the curriculum, both in its own right and as part of a much-needed national debate about culture, society and identity.'

Thus one of the principal objectives in this book is to articulate what should be the best history learning experiences possible to engage all the various pupils taking history at school and speak to their needs both as young people and future citizens.

The second objective relates to the realisation of the first: how can history be effectively taught through the framework of the statutory Order for history? To understand what different pupils can achieve at successive stages of their development and how, indeed, they may be helped to progress in knowledge, skills and understanding must be at the heart of good teaching. Everyone involved in schools agrees, as Blatchford and Howard have observed, that continuity in learning and teaching is 'a good thing'. Moreover, progression is referred to in most HMI reports on schools; it is integral to effective schools' development planning; and, as a result of the introduction of the National Curriculum, it has increasingly become the focus of INSET provision (Blatchford and Howard, 1993). Nevertheless, very little has been written from a subject perspective although the National Curriculum was originally planned with continuity and progression in mind and its subject-based Orders were intended to establish a framework for learning from 5 to 16 and beyond. Such a framework, however, is no longer fully in place for history and geography. If, under the 'Dearing' curriculum a large number of children will experience most of their history teaching in the primary school, liaison between teachers and schools becomes increasingly important if pupils are to progress steadily and their achievements, however tenuous, to be built upon. Many teachers are anxious to have greater knowledge of good practice across the key stages of schooling and to improve their teaching as a result, but such evidence is not easily available. If there is not to be a discontinuity in learning, teaching resources are needed to supply the previous deficiencies. This book seeks to be amongst the first since the new Order for history to do so.

Chapter 1 offers a defence of history's position in the school curriculum. This defence is structured around issues of 'pupil entitlement' and the teaching and learning of history. The chapter develops an argument which teachers can use to hold and enhance the place of history in the curriculum. To begin with, therefore, the book looks at what pupils are entitled to in terms of what has actually been promised in official thinking and our reflections on what they should be entitled to in their experience of history in schools. Once we know this we can work out what we want children to progress in.

The following chapter documents our current understanding of what we mean by progression in history. It examines what seemed to be said about this in the 1991 Order and how this has been affected by the revised Order of 1995. The value is recognised of all the research which has been undertaken as a result of the implications of the National Curriculum and the problems that teachers had to face in implementing an artificial, hierarchical ladder of attainment. Some planning strategies for making progression a reality in the learning experiences of children 5 to 16 are then considered.

For pupils to progress satisfactorily, it is important to examine liaison across the key stages, how it has been managed, what problems there might be and how they could be overcome. Real progression cannot take place if at the beginning of each key stage the previous experiences of children in history and the knowledge, understanding and skills they have built up, are ignored. This is true too of the type of learning. For example Key Stage 1 to Key Stage 2 takes children from their own memory to official memory and from individual to social to national memory; from experiential to factual accounts. These are different animals, constructed on different premises (Fentress and Wickham, 1992). The exciting, engaging work in Key Stage 1 is individual affirming but Key Stage 2 frightens year three with empirical study. These difficulties hamper progression from Key Stage 1 to Key Stage 2. On the other hand, since the teaching of history in the primary school has improved so much since the advent of the National Curriculum it is vital that secondary teachers know and utilise what their pupils bring with them. As Sue Bardwell shows this is true of all stages but there are many difficulties in the way of successful liaison. Carefully thought-out profiling is one of the solutions that is offered here.

Undoubtedly progression needs to be considered across knowledge, skills and understanding but some of the main areas where this can be developed throughout the key stages and into GCSE have been relatively neglected. This might continue to be so in the new Order unless attention is drawn to them. Subtle changes of wording throughout the level descriptions do depict the pupils' growing understanding of the complexity of human attitudes and beliefs and of the different features of past societies. The latter comprise the old attainment target 1c, the target which most helped pupils to appreciate the depth, richness and variety of history and the difficulty of making pat or simplistic judgements about the past. Attainment target 1c interwove so much with the other attainment targets, especially the use of sources, that it was difficult to separate them and, crucially, it was the focus which linked those very important aspects of the programmes of study – diversity and the experiences of men and women – to the skills and understanding of history. These strands are present in the new attainment target but they are less clearly worded and somewhat lost in the middle of comprehensive level descriptions. More importantly they appear in the Key Element 'range and depth of historical knowledge and understanding' but although progression is indicated across the three key stages, more detailed exposition might be vital if teachers are to pay attention to these areas.

It is recognised in the new Order that knowledge needs to become deeper, broader, better selected, linked, analysed and explained and this in the context of increasing independence of enquiry and critical use of sources. The problem of how to tie subject matter with the Key Elements and then to consider significant issues and explore them at different stages in increasing depth and complexity provides the focus for the next three chapters. Strategies are offered through a consideration of several issues which are of prime importance (although controversial and/or neglected) across the key stages to 16. These are how to build up knowledge and understanding of 'British' history, cultural diversity and gender issues.

Paul Bracey examines what we mean by 'British' and what are the statutory requirements on 'British' history. He gives examples of how, through understanding of the concept of 'British', chronological development, ideas of change, and continuity can be built up. Peter Rogers probes the entire issue of the teaching of cultural diversity in history, emphasising that it is crucially a matter which must be considered by the senior management and, indeed, the whole school if individual teachers are to be able to tackle it successfully. Further he locates the debate about cultural diversity in the curriculum in the context of a fast-changing world. Gender issues are equally important – women are equally part of history with men although their under-representation in history books (and, often, teaching) would not seem to support this and probably does much to reinforce old prejudices. Understanding is needed throughout the history curriculum both of women's participation and their differences in experience. As Erica Pounce points out, it would help if notions of this were built on from the beginning rather than merely having a statutory chapter in each study unit.

The various skills of enquiry and communication, so crucial to developing real understanding of the subject, are interrelated with these but also deserve a separate chapter. Pupils need to learn to ask as a matter of course questions about the past, its evidence, perspectives, diversity and interpretations. The experience of teachers would suggest that interest, involvement and motivation are key factors in stimulating them to ask such questions naturally and this is more likely to happen if teachers are constantly taking them back to issues they have met before and using pupils' previous understanding and knowledge (including their personal experience) to reinforce, develop and expand their views. (This does, of course, presuppose that teachers within departments know what and how pupils have learnt before). It is welcome that enquiry and source work are now linked. This is much more in line with what historians do and with good teaching and learning.

History can be communicated in many ways – pictures, posters, maps, diagrams, charts, stories, narrative, notes, essays, oral accounts, role-play, drama, IT, tape, video. Oral work can become as important in GCSE and A level as earlier in a pupil's career. Language development is important. It is often pointed out that history is difficult for those not proficient in English but history can be a vehicle for developing English; it builds up concept development and ways of communicating, including different ways of writing and giving oral communication as well as visual representation.

Any of the skills identified above, which are central to being a successful young historian, can be developed individually, in pairs, groups, or in classes. However, these skills, as Chris Palmer demonstrates, will not be developed in a progressive way over the years unless they are planned for, monitored and reviewed in schemes of work.

Such development obviously needs to be taken through to 14–16, the original entitlement for all children for history, and, indeed, beyond to 16–18. The loss of statutory history from 14 to 16 has been serious enough for the status of the subject and for the coherence of the rest of the statutory history Orders without this being compounded by learning at this age not building on the skills and understanding developed before. In many secondary schools such liaison should not be difficult even if the teachers of the pupils aged over 14 are not those who taught them at 11–14. Clearly, whatever the apparent difficulties of the original Key Stage 4 and however the new Order seeks to overcome the castration of history, there is a discontinuity now in subject matter between post 14 and

6

Key Stage 3. Furthermore, Key Stages 1, 2 and 3 are not externally assessed but GCSE and A level are. Does this mean that in secondary schools heads of department in particular might have pressures in their history teaching which are different from the National Curriculum and might even pull against it? If levels of response stay in GCSE assessment, for example, how will this affect continuity between it and Key Stage 3 (see, for example, White, 1992,). Similar questions have to be asked about effects of A level on GCSE or if history becomes involved in GNVQs.

How far this affects planning for progression in skills and understanding depends on how much the GCSE criteria match the Key Elements and level descriptions of the National Curriculum. SCAA has explicitly aimed for such continuity and the terminology of the latest proposals for GCSE criteria have moved markedly closer to that of the National Curriculum (although, if anything, more to that of the 1991-4 Order than the new) and with some subtle differences echo level descriptions 8, 9 and 10 of the old Order. Only level 8 has been retained in the new Order now that history is statutory only to 14 although there is a level for 'exceptional performance'. Both these give an explicit demonstration of what pupils might be able to achieve and a necessary overlap into GCSE-type work.

The Key Elements are reflected in GCSE too: in particular, understanding of how historical interpretations differ is an assessment objective whilst each syllabus has to look at history both from a variety of perspectives and at the 'social, cultural, religious and ethnic diversity of the societies studied and the experiences of men and women in [them]' (SCAA, 1994m). These syllabus directives are not spelt out so explicitly in the other parts of the document but, nevertheless, they are there. They appear again in the new subject core for A/AS history where, as James Kilmartin will show, much of the terminology is readily recognisable by those familiar with the National Curriculum. Thus in A level too an appropriate range of skills is being tested and some boards are recognising history as an active subject by including a personal study.

In short, this book is about ensuring that children enjoy coherent learning experiences which recognise the intellectual, cultural and social benefits to children engaging with the study of history.

History is, above all, a questioning activity. Each new generation of academic historians, as Christopher Hill observed, 'asks new questions of the past, finds new areas of sympathy as it relives different aspects of its predecessors' (Kaye, 1992). Similarly, in a democratic society each new generation of school leavers should be empowered to question received readings of the past. Such skills, as argued above and throughout this book, need to be developed progressively throughout the school history curriculum. Moreover, such skills are critical for the future of democracy for it is still possible for a DFE official to declare:

> 'We are in a period of considerable social change. There may be social unrest, but we can cope with the Toxteths. But if we have a highly educated and idle population we may possibly anticipate more serious social conflict. People must be educated once more to know their place.' (Simon, 1988)

If, however, such skills in critical thinking in history as elucidated in this book could be built up in young people, such a submissive society could not be so easily achieved.

1

Pupil entitlement and the teaching and learning of history

Ian Grosvenor and Ruth Watts

Since the late 1960s texts focusing on the teaching and learning of history in schools have generally conformed to a pattern. There is usually a philosophical discourse on the 'nature of history' followed by a passionate justification of the subject's place in the curriculum. This approach has emerged in the context of perceived threats to the subject's classroom survival: the debate over relevance, the pretensions of social studies and humanities programmes, the curriculum shift to greater vocationalism. It should, therefore, come as no surprise to find history once more under threat in schools. History has survived previous assaults, but the prognosis for the subject's survival in the second half of the 1990s can only be described as grim: history's place in the 5–16 curriculum continuum has been cut by a quarter; from September 1995 the subject's relevance for all children will be deemed to end at 14. This downgrading of history's importance in the curriculum will inevitably place the subject at risk in the earlier key stages as curriculum managers review time and resource allocations. This chapter, in line with tradition, will seek to defend history's curriculum position. However, this defence will depart from traditional argument in that it will be framed around issues of 'pupil entitlement' and the teaching and learning of history. The concept of entitlement will be used to explore the possibilities of developing an argument which will enable teachers not only to hold, but also to enhance, history's position in the school curriculum. Further, while nothing can be done at present about history's optional status in Key Stage 4, the entitlement argument will hopefully also be of value to those teachers engaged in making the case for the provision of GCSE history in their schools.

Pupil entitlement surfaced as part of educational vocabulary in the 1980s. Its usage was generally linked to curriculum reform (Chitty, 1988). In 1983 HMI produced a report on the curriculum 11–16 which presented the case for a synthesis of the vocational, the technical and the academic into an 'entitlement curriculum':

'It seemed essential that all pupils should be guaranteed a curriculum of a distinctive breadth and depth to which they should be *entitled,* irrespective of the type of school they attended or level of ability or their social circumstances and that failure to provide such a curriculum is unacceptable.' (DES, 1983)

Four years later entitlement was at the centre of government curriculum reform and the concept was extended to include the primary sector. *The National Curriculum 5–16: A Consultation Document* stated that **all** pupils:

'should be entitled to...the same good and relevant curriculum and programmes of study which include the key content, skills and processes which they need to learn and which ensure that the content and teaching of the various elements of the national curriculum bring out their relevance to and links with pupils' own experiences and their practical applications and continuing value to adult and working life.' (DES, 1987)

The principle of 'entitlement' was enshrined in law in 1988: pupils were to have access to 'a balanced and broadly based curriculum' which promoted their 'spiritual, moral, cultural, mental and physical development' and that 'of society' as a whole and prepared them for 'the opportunities, responsibilities and experiences of adult life' (Education Reform Act, 1988). In 1989 the DES again drew attention to the significance of the idea of entitlement, when in *From Policy into Practice* it issued headteachers and governors with guidance on the production of school development plans to help implement the requirements of the Education Act :'[the Act] entitles every pupil to a curriculum which is broad and balanced' (DES, 1989).

Thus, entitlement was associated in official thinking with the content, skills and processes of curriculum subjects 5–16; with their relevance to and application in, the 'real world'; with curriculum breadth and balance, and, implicitly,with 'good' classroom delivery. How did these principles of entitlement inform the development of National Curriculum history?

Direct references to pupil entitlement have been few in documentation relating to the teaching of National Curriculum history. *The National Curriculum History Working Group: Final Report* (DES, 1990a), from which the 1991 Statutory Order was derived, did not explicitly refer to 'pupil entitlement', but instead offered a general rationale for school history. The Working Group listed nine 'purposes' of school history:

- To help understand the present in the context of the past. There is nothing in the present that cannot be better understood in the light of its historical context and origins.
- To arouse interest in the past. History naturally arouses curiosity, raises fundamental questions, and generates speculation.
- To give pupils a sense of identity. Through history pupils can learn about the origins and story of their family and of other groups to which they belong, of their community and country, and of institutions, beliefs, values, customs, and underlying shared assumptions.
- To help give pupils an understanding of their own cultural roots and shared inheritances. No standard, uniform culture can be imposed on the young in so culturally diverse a society as exists in Britain, yet much is shared in common. Although questions about the origins and nature of British culture are complex, school history can put shared inheritances in their historical context.
- To contribute to pupils' knowledge and understanding of other countries and other cultures in the modern world. Education in British society should be rooted in toleration and respect for cultural variety. Studying the history of other societies from their own perspectives and for their own sake counteracts tendencies to insularity, without devaluing British achievements, values and traditions.
- To train the mind by means of disciplined study. History relies heavily upon disciplined enquiry, systematic analysis and evaluation, argument, logical rigour and a search for the truth.
- To introduce pupils to the distinctive methodology of historians. Historians attempt to construct their own coherent accounts of the past by the rigorous testing of evidence which is often incomplete; the skills involved in doing this have benefits beyond the study of history.
- To enrich other areas of the curriculum. History draws on the record of the entire human past; it is a subject of immense breadth which can both inform, and draw upon, other areas of the curriculum.
- To prepare pupils for adult life. History gives pupils a framework of reference, opportunities for the informed use of leisure, and a critically sharpened intelligence with which to make sense of current affairs. History is a priceless preparation for citizenship, work, and leisure. It encourages pupils to approach them from angles not considered by other subjects or forms of study in the curriculum.

The Working Group recognised that not all of the 'purposes' taken individually applied only to the study of history in school, but taken together they argued the nine purposes 'are what makes history unique'. The Working Group expanded on the curricular implications of these 'purposes' in the third chapter of their report where they considered what constituted 'the essence of history'. The study of history, they stated, should involve pupils in the 'acquisition of knowledge as understanding' within a chronological framework, in having 'respect' for evidence and the pursuit of historical objectivity, and in understanding that 'there are no monopolies of the truth'. Thus, there was a clear link between their understanding of the fundamental purposes of school history and the realisation of these 'purposes' in the classroom, or to put it another way, with the 'doing' of history in schools. These 'purposes', and their realisation in the classroom, apply to **all** pupils. It logically follows, therefore, that the statements regarding the purposes of school history and the essence of history can implicitly be read as statements of pupil entitlement.

This implicit relationship between 'purpose', 'doing' and 'entitlement' became almost explicit in the section of the report where the Group outlined their criteria for the selection of historical content. Employing the language of earlier DES pronouncements on the entitlement curriculum, the Working Group stated that the history curriculum had to reflect both 'breadth' and 'balance'. The content should:

- pay attention to the various dimensions of the study of history (political; economic, technological and scientific; social and religious; cultural and aesthetic);
- provide a balance of historical periods: ancient, medieval and modern;
- offer a good balance of local, national and world history;
- [offer] a wide range of perspectives:...of the rich, the poor, of men and of women, of different ethnic groups, of particular ideologies in their human context;
- [include] different spans of historical study;
- give opportunities for different interpretations and illustrate a range of points of view;
- help...pupils to raise fundamental questions about human society;
- introduce pupils to a range of their historical inheritances;
- develop a wide range of skills derived from historical methodology.

History in the National Curriculum (England) (DES, 1991) omitted all direct references to the purpose and essence of history in schools and focused instead on presenting a minimalist set of statements relating to the attainment targets and the programmes of study. As with the report of the Working Group, there were no direct references to pupil entitlement.

Nevertheless, entitlement was clearly implied with regard to both skills and content:

> 'The attainment targets and their constituent statements of attainment, specify the knowledge, skills and understanding which pupils of different abilities and maturities are expected to have by the end of each key stage. The programmes of study specify the matters, skills and processes to be taught to pupils.' (DES, 1991)

In other words (and perhaps to state the obvious) the Order listed the historical knowledge, skills and understanding which **all** pupils were **expected** to **have** and the matters, skills and processes which **had to be taught**. This entitlement was statutory. A concern with issues relating to pupil entitlement can also be found in the text which frames the 30 constituent statements of attainment and the key stage content specific statements of the Order. It is here, in the framing text, that the Working Group's ideas about the 'doing' of history were translated into unambiguous statements about the types of classroom experiences which all pupils should enjoy. These experiences are usually preceded by the phrase 'pupils should be given opportunities to…'. These opportunities, which number 27, were to function across the 4 key stages.

Across the four key stages pupils should have opportunities to:

- explore links between history and other subjects;
- develop information technology capability;
- develop knowledge, understanding and skills related to cross-curricular themes;
- develop a sense of chronology;
- use words and phrases relating to the passage of time;
- develop an awareness of the past and the ways in which it was different to the present;
- investigate and describe historical change;
- examine different types of cause and consequence;
- observe, analyse and make connections between different features of historical situations;
- develop awareness of interpetations of past events;
- develop understanding of how the selection of historical information can influence interpretations;
- analyse the ways in which the past can be represented;
- use a range of historical sources;
- select, analyse, compare and evaluate historical sources;
- investigate historical topics on their own;
- ask questions about the past;

- choose sources for an investigation;
- collect and record information;
- communicate awareness and understanding of history orally, visually and in writing;
- study different types of past events;
- study history from a variety of perspectives;
- investigate local history;
- study the social, cultural, religious and ethnic diversity of societies;
- study the experiences of men and women;
- study the ideas, beliefs and attitudes of people in different societies;
- develop awareness of how the histories of Britain, Europe and the world are linked;
- (through their historical studies) prepare themselves for citizenship, work and leisure (DES, 1991).

Where the phrase 'pupil entitlement' did appear in history specific curriculum documents it reflected the Order's emphasis on knowledge, understanding, skills and the opportunity to 'do' history. Thus, National Curriculum Council (NCC) INSET materials for Key Stage 3 included a section on balancing differentiation and 'entitlement for all':

'the needs of different pupils should be balanced with the entitlement of all pupils to a broad, balanced experience of history. The study units make no reference to differentiation; they are an outline of historical information which all pupils are entitled to, irrespective of their ability....The PoS defines a common entitlement, while the SoA suggest how this can be differentiated. Teachers may wish to make a distinction between entitlement and differentiation in their schemes of work.' (NCC, 1993c)

To reinforce this point the NCC included a diagram to show the relationship between pupil entitlement and methods of differentiation. Three key statements can be extracted from this diagram:

- **Knowledge entitlement** – by the end of the unit all pupils should have an outline knowledge of:...
- **Concepts entitlement** – by the end of the unit pupils should be aware of the following concepts and terms...
- **Attainment entitlement** – all pupils should undertake work on...by the end of the unit they should all be able to...

It is clear that for NCC officers entitlement in history was related to pupils having access to the knowledge, concepts and terminology integral to the succesful completion of a unit of work and also to the opportunities for demonstrating attainment.

The principles of entitlement which were clearly integral to the philosophy behind the Working Group's *Final Report,* the Statutory Order and subsequent NCC INSET materials are also implicit in the criteria published by the regulatory body OFSTED with regard to the inspection of schools in general and history provision in particular (OFSTED, 1993a,b). Issues of entitlement clearly underpin the evaluative criteria relating to standards of achievement, quality of learning and quality of teaching. These criteria are presented in an evaluative framework, but can easily be re-cast in terms of statements of pupil entitlement in the history classroom. Pupils are **entitled to learning experiences** which allow them to demonstrate their:

- progress in knowledge and understanding of history;
- ability to give historical explanations;
- ability to investigate and work with historical sources of different kinds;
- ability to provide interpretations of the past which are consistent with the evidence;
- ability to locate, select and organise historical information;
- ability to present findings appropriately and effectively give historical explanations;
- sense of the past;
- awareness of how the past has helped to fashion the present;
- enthusiasm for exploring the past;
- respect for evidence;
- toleration of a range of opinions;
- constructive approach to collaborative working.

For OFSTED there is a clear correlation between pupils' learning experiences and the quality of teaching they receive. Again adapting OFSTED evaluative criteria, it can also be argued that pupils are **entitled to teaching** where:

- lessons have clear objectives;
- pupils are aware of these objectives;
- teachers have a secure command of the subject;
- lessons have suitable content;
- activities are well chosen to promote learning of that content;
- activities are presented in ways which will engage, motivate and challenge all pupils;
- fieldwork, visits and simulations are used wherever possible;
- there is an abundance of books, documents, newspapers, records, maps,

photographs, artefacts, and sound and video recordings available to support the teaching, provide evidence and form the basis for practical work.

This list obviously goes well beyond ideas about entitlement as implied or stated in other National Curriculum documentation. However, it does provide a partial explanation for the observable gap between principles of pupil entitlement and curriculum reality which has characterised National Curriculum history as experienced by pupils over the last few years. This gap, it is generally acknowledged, can be attributed in part to a lack of teacher understanding of the issues, coupled with a lack of effective INSET. However, the main reason for this gap between curriculum principles and reality lay with the intrinsic difficulties of content overload and an unrealistic hierarchy of assessment objectives (Grosvenor and Watts, 1993).

What, then, of the new Order, to what extent has the entitlement for pupils with regard to teaching and learning of history been modified? The answer is very simple. The principles of entitlement, developed since the late 1980s and documented above are, in the main, intact. The new Order, in this sense, clearly represents a commitment to continuity. The areas of omission relate to links between history and other subjects and cross-curricular themes. In the new Order pupil entitlement is integral to each key stage focus statement, to the content defined for each key stage, and to the areas of progression in pupils' historical knowledge, understanding and skills identified in the five Key Elements: chronology; range and depth of historical understanding; interpretations of history; historical enquiry; organisation and communication. Furthermore, pupil entitlement is also implicit in the Level Descriptions. Each description 'provides an overview of key features of typical performance at that level and provides the basis for judgements about a pupil's performance' (SCAA,1994b).

Pupils have to be given, and are entitled to, the opportunity to demonstrate their knowledge, understanding and skills. What has changed, however, is the amount of time available to realise this entitlement. History is now compulsory only between the ages of 5 and 14 years. Dearing could see no 'reason, either nationally or in terms of the individual student' for the study of history to be a statutory requirement in Key Stage 4 (Dearing, 1994). This constitutes a profound shift away from a common curriculum for all as embodied in the Education Reform Act. Curricular differentiation will now characterise Key Stage 4. Further, as a consequence of National Curriculum history ending at age 14, levels 9 and 10, which were equivalent to GCSE A grades, have disappeared to be replaced by a broad statement about exceptional performance. The new

Order has also reduced the content to be covered and made exemplary, rather than statutory, some of the types of events pupils need to be taught about. The total extent of the revisions to school history can be readily comprehended: the Programmes of Study and Attainment Targets in the 'old' Order totalled 54 pages, in the 'new' they are presented in less than 20 pages (DES, 1991; DFE, 1995). What are the consequences of such changes for pupil entitlement? What will be the backwash effect of history's optional status after 14 on the earlier key stages? Indeed, can pupil entitlement in history be realised and sustained under the new curriculum framework? To answer these questions attention will now focus on four areas which directly impinge on the issue of pupil entitlement: curriculum time, curriculum planning, curriculum content, and teacher subject knowledge.

The revised national curriculum is not a complete curriculum. It occupies 80% of curriculum time in key stages 1–3. The implementation of Dearing's revised curriculum requires governing bodies to make curriculum policy decisions about how the discretionary 20% is used. Dearing recommended that the priorities for the use of this time should be to support work in the basics of literacy, oracy and numeracy, work in 'those National Curriculum subjects which the school chooses to explore in more depth', and in Key Stage 3, for sex education and careers education and guidance (Dearing, 1994). Personal and social education, cross-curricular themes, revised syllabuses in religious education and other non-National Curriculum subjects will also be competing for this time. Whatever choice governing bodies make, and of course all policy decisions should be open to regular review, they must account to parents for their decision in the governors' annual reports.

History, as already stated, is no longer compulsory after 14. It follows that history's academic coherence and rigour cannot be sustained in the remaining key stages if curriculum time allocated to the subject is not protected and, indeed, enhanced. This point was, in part, recognised by Dearing in relation to the 20% optional time in Key Stage 3: 'schools will clearly need to devote the bulk of the 20% optional time to the ten National Curriculum subjects if standards in GCSE and other public examinations are to be sustained'. It also follows, therefore, that **as a minimum** the notional time allocated to history (although not prescribed) by Dearing in his review, of one hour a week in Key Stage 1 and 75 minutes in Key Stages 2 and 3 has to be accepted and incorporated into curriculum plans as a norm if the subject is to be studied as an academic discipline (Dearing, 1994). It is worth noting here, that in some schools this time allocation would be an advance on what was happening under the old National Curriculum framework (Grosvenor and Watts, 1993).

History *Update,* which was issued simultaneously with the draft of the new history Order by SCAA, took the issue of curriculum time a stage further and made a clear case for curriculum time enhancement across all three key stages: 'the areas of study constitute a pupil's minimum entitlement in history'. Teachers can, of course, add additional units or extend the scope of the prescribed units (SCAA, 1994c). Such advice provides useful support for teachers of history engaged in negotiations with curriculum planners and governing bodies. However, it might equally be objected that such advice represents the vested interests of the SCAA officers for history, that the subject's relevance is doubtful given its optional status in Key Stage 4, and its case for more curriculum time is no stronger than any other curriculum area. It is at this point, in making a bid for curriculum time, that the issue of pupil entitlement becomes critical.

The principles of pupil entitlement documented above were conceived and developed in the understanding that history was to be taught across the years of compulsory schooling. This is no longer the case. Therefore, in terms of pupil entitlement in history it is surely a truism to say that what was to be achieved over 11 years of compulsory schooling cannot be readily achieved in 9 years. If the underlying principles have remained the same, but the amount of time available to realise these principles has been cut, then history will have to be allocated more time across all three stages if pupil entitlement is to be a reality and the quality of children's learning of history sustained. To this end, all the statements still in force relating to pupil entitlement are brought together below as an *aide-mémoire* for presenting the case for history's share of the 20% discretionary time. It could be objected that some of the areas of pupil entitlement identified fall outside the learning experiences associated with Key Stage 1 classrooms. This position is untenable. Curriculum experiences do not happen in isolation, they build on and extend previous experiences. If this does not happen there can be no progression.

Pupil entitlement and National Curriculum history: *an aide-mémoire*

Across the three key stages pupils should have opportunities to:

- develop an awareness of the past in outline and in depth;
- study history from a variety of perspectives;
- study the histories of England, Ireland, Scotland and Wales;
- study the history of Britain in its European and world context;
- study local history;

- make links and connections between events;
- study events, people and changes in chronological framework;
- use dates, terms and conventions relating to historical periods and the passing of time;
- investigate and assess change;
- describe, analyse and explain causes and conseqences;
- identify differences between ways of life at different times;
- use stories from different periods and cultures;
- study the ideas, beliefs and attitudes of people in the past;
- study the experiences of men and women in the past;
- study the social, cultural, religious and ethnic diversity of societies in the past;
- identify, analyse and evaluate different ways in which the past is represented;
- investigate and work independently with historical sources of different kinds;
- ask and answer questions;
- locate, select and organise historical information;
- communicate their awareness and understanding of history in a variety of ways;
- express themselves clearly in both speech and writing;
- develop and apply their information technology capability.

Before leaving the issue of curriculum time, it is important to outline briefly an additional argument for access to discretionary time which can be deployed to complement that focusing on issues of entitlement. This argument relates to curriculum strategies to realise one of the central requirements of the 1988 Education Reform Act: pupils' spiritual, moral, social and cultural development. Towards the end of John Patten's time as Education Secretary he attacked young people for having:

'too little understanding of our democratic and cultural heritage.... Knowledge and understanding should be linked to the conscious growth of moral values and codes...as they apply to dealings with individuals and institutions. This should include what it means to be a British citizen, whether by birth or settlement.' (Grosvenor, 1994)

This criticism of British youth was followed a month later by an OFSTED consultation document which sought to identify a 'prospectus' of spiritual, moral, social and cultural learning outcomes in schools which could be monitored. These learning outcomes included:

- **Knowledge of**:
- the central beliefs, ideas and practices of major world religions and philosophies;
- the language of ideas and morality;
- the ways in which societies function and are organised;
- the nature and roots of their own cultural traditions and practices and other major cultural groups within their own society.

- **Understanding of**:
- how people have sought to explain the universe through various myths and stories, including religious, historical and scientific interpretations;
- the nature and purposes of moral discussion; the diversity of religious, social, aesthetic, ethnic and political traditions;
- how individuals relate to each other and to the institutions, structures and processes of society.

- **Personal values in relation to**: the self, relationship with others (tolerance, respect, compassion etc..), local, national and world issues (war and peace, human rights, exploitation, equal opportunities etc.) (OFSTED, 1994).

Obviously, history will not be alone in contributing to these developments in school, but it must surely be the lead subject if this list of outcomes is read against the purposes of school history given above and the statements in the entitlement *aide-mémoire*. Further, if the lead role of history is accepted, Dearing's decision to make history optional in Key Stage 4 becomes incomprehensible in this context. Consequently, history's claim to discretionary time in the earlier key stages can only be strengthened. Similarly, history's suitability as a curriculum vehicle for developing oracy, literacy, numeracy, and the cross-curricular themes not covered in the OFSTED discussion paper cannot be underestimated (Baldwin, 1994; Curtis and Bardwell, 1994; Haydn, 1994; Hoodless, 1994; Isaac, 1994; DES, 1985). As Sir Keith Joseph observed in 1984:

'The knowledge, understanding and skills which the study of history can confer are of great value in themselves. To acquire an interest in the past is itself a cultural acquisition which can enrich the whole of one's adult life.... In addition history can...encourage young people to use their reason as well as their memories. It can develop skills of analysis and criticism...by encouraging pupils to evaluate primary source material...the skills acquired through the study of history can also enhance young people's use of language, numeracy, observation and communication with other people. History is indispensable to understanding the society we live in.... In short, history, properly taught, justifies its place in the curriculum by what it does to prepare all pupils for the responsibilities of citizenship.' (Joseph,1984)

It is worth stating, perhaps with hindsight, that it was extremely unfortunate for history's future as a school subject that the rancour and polemic of the knowledge versus skills debate in the late 1980s and early 1990s served in some ways to mask the pivotal role of history in a democratic society.

The next two issues, curriculum planning and content, require only brief comment as they provide the focus for subsequent chapters in this book. The demands of pupil entitlement clearly require attention to be carefully directed towards pedagogy and assessment both within and across the key stages if entitlement is to be realised. As HMI stated in 1989: 'the 5–16 curriculum is constructed and delivered as a continuous and coherent whole, in which the primary phase prepares for the secondary phase, and the latter builds on the former' (HMI, 1989). Teachers will have to plan if pupil entitlement in history is to be a classroom reality. In this sense, the *aide-mémoire* on entitlement can also be regarded as an instrument for curriculum review and planning. It is perhaps pertinent at this point to note that a core of the entitlement statements listed above are also in evidence in the GCSE Criteria for History and in the A/AS Core for History. The compulsory history curriculum may end at 14, but there is clear progression in terms of entitlement through to GCSE and to advanced level study.

In terms of curriculum content, the reduction in the amount of history to be studied coupled with the subject's optional status at Key Stage 4 clearly poses potential problems for realising pupil entitlement. The criticism levelled at the original National Curriculum for history that it was a politicised curriculum which offered pupils a selective reading of the past still stands. However, the distinction between core and supplementary units has been removed and the historical content which is listed constitutes 'a pupil's minimum entitlement in history' (SCAA, 1994b,c). Thus, there is much greater scope for teacher professional judgement about what can be taught and the emphasis given than under the old Statutory Order. As Robin Alexander observed it 'is not the Orders but what teachers and children do with them' that matters (Alexander, 1994). In short, the potential to realise pupil entitlement is there, but it is up to teachers to make it happen.

This chapter has documented what might be termed the 'official' or 'professional' view of pupil entitlement in history as it has emerged since the late 1980s. This same period also witnessed a certain confusion emerging amongst historians as to the purpose and nature of historical enquiry. There have been debates over the challenge posed by post-modernism, over claims about 'the End of History' following the collapse of international communism and with it the conventional narrative structure for twentieth century history, and disagreements over the primacy of competing perspectives and narratives of Britain's past. School history will not, indeed has not, been immune from the effects of this confusion and uncertainty. The question, therefore, has to be posed: to what extent does, or will, this confusion and uncertainty undermine the arguments about entitlement presented here? At the centre of the History Working Group's understanding of what the study of history involved was a recognition that 'there are no monopolies of the truth'. This premise provided the foundation for Attainment Target 2. It is central to the Key Elements of the new Order and, the present writers would argue, is at the heart of pupil entitlement. In a post-Cold War world, in a post-modern world, in a world where competing narratives of the past and their bearing on the future jostle each other for primacy, the recognition that 'there are no monopolies of the truth' and the acceptance that this is part of a child's learning entitlement is critical. However, like all learning objectives it needs to be planned for if it is to be realised. 'Telling the truth about history', to borrow Appleby, Hunt and Jacob's phrase, requires teachers to plan learning experiences which offer a plurality of narratives and intepretations (Appleby, Hunt and Jacob, 1994). Pupils are entitled to be know 'the truth about history', it is only then that they will develop a 'positive reflexive scepticism' towards the past (Jenkins, 1991). In short, if pupils are denied 'the truth about history' they will not experience a balanced curriculum. This observation brings the analysis to the final issue raised above, that of teacher subject knowledge.

John Slater has observed that teachers of history need not only 'to understand what history is and how it is learnt, but what it is *for*'. The task of history teacher educators, he continued, was 'to help students place their craft in a modest historical, sociological and *philosophical* context' (Slater, 1993). The new criteria and procedures in England and Wales for accrediting courses of initial teacher education are based on a competence model. There is an implicit danger in this model that prospective teachers will be trained, but not educated; trained to teach, to impart subject knowledge, but not to reflect and critically evaluate teaching and learning processes. As Dave Hill has forcefully argued, the competence based regulations for the initial education of teachers have the potential to limit courses to 'a non-critical instruction and training in how to "deliver", uncritically' the National Curriculum (Hill, 1994). The demands of competence development and the need to demonstrate evidence of capability for a competence profile will severely restrict the amount of time available for student teachers to reflect on the nature of history, to understand that historical knowledge is constructed and always provisional and to engage with a plurality of historical narratives and interpretations.

This issue becomes even more critical when the full implications of the decision to end the compulsory nature of history as a National Curriculum subject at 14 are taken into account. A significant number of children will, from now on, experience the bulk of their education in history during their primary years. Some teachers will enter the primary sector with a degree in history and a PGCE. However, it is not necessarily the case that such teachers will have experienced Slater's 'modest historical, sociological and philosophical context' in their undergraduate degree and the amount of time available to them to consider such issues on PGCE courses is negligible. Student teachers on a three year B.Ed degree (soon likely to become the norm), with an increased school-based element, and with the subject demands of the whole primary curriculum to assimilate, will equally find the time to reflect critically about history limited. The Dearing curriculum changes will reduce the range and volume of work to be covered, but as HMI Richards noted the primary National Curriculum will 'still be demanding for both teachers and pupils' (Richards, 1994).

What, then, of pupil entitlement to 'the truth about history'? The answer has, at present, to be the same as that given by Mao Tse-Tung when asked about the influence of the French Revolution: 'it is too soon to say'. Certainly, recognising that there is a problem constitutes half the solution. Teacher education is set to go through a tumultuous period of change. The shift to competence-based teacher education is not going to go away; competence and capability are part of the changing policy environment of the 1990s in all areas of education and training (HEQC, 1994). In the development of new forms of partnership between teacher educators and school-based mentors, issues relating to pupil entitlement and, in particular, strategies for promoting student reflection and critical thinking, **must be discussed**, **planned and regularly reviewed together**. Further, as good practice emerges it must be disseminated as widely as possible.

This chapter will end with a tale of two knights, one of whom defended what was good and important and one who saw what was good but did not recognise its importance. In 1984 Sir Keith Joseph stated that history was:

'an essential component in the curriculum of *all* pupils...it should be present throughout the primary and secondary phases up to the age 16: and this should be made explicit in any future statements of curricular objectives for the primary as well as for the secondary phase. I stress this point because it is sometimes suggested that to secure that breadth in the curriculum, that nearly everyone thinks desirable, it would be enough to guarantee that each child studied a humanity; that geography, say, or economics might be substituted for history. Those other humanities bring their own unique perspectives and have their own distinctive role in preparing pupils for adult life and work.... But they are not a substitute for history.' (Joseph, 1984)

In Sir Ron Dearing's final report on the National Curriculum he stated that:

'History and geography are absorbing and valuable subjects. But I cannot see a reason, either nationally or in terms of the individual student, why these subjects should, as a matter of law, be given priority in this key stage over others, such as the creative arts, a second foreign language, home economics, the classics, religious studies, business studies or economics. I recommend, therefore, that they should be optional in Key Stage 4.' (Dearing, 1994)

It is ironic that before making this recommendation Dearing drew on the historical record to frame his report. He used history to offer the contextual framework for all that followed:

'"Upon the education of the people of this country, the future of this country depends."

If this was true when Disraeli spoke these words in 1874 when Britain was at the height of its economic power, it is even more so today. In a highly competitive world there is nowhere to hide.... We should not take risks with the education of millions of pupils. My personal accountability to these pupils means that I must be confident that the case for any change is well-founded.' (Dearing, 1994)

And the moral of this tale – 10 years is a long time in history!

2

Progression in Children's Learning in History

Ruth Watts and Ian Grosvenor

The underlying theme of this book is progression in the learning of history throughout compulsory schooling. It is looking at not just how children **think** in history but how to help them **progress** from where they are at a given point to what it may be hoped they can do at another. The points made in Chapter 1 about the value of history and what pupils are entitled to are the focus throughout. In seeking to achieve progression not only will the National Curriculum, which covers the ages 5 to 14, be considered but also GCSE and whether this builds on what has gone before. This chapter will first examine the meaning of progression in the learning of history, then how far the National Curriculum, the post-Dearing changes and GCSE respectively have enabled the type of progression desired or, indeed, any at all and lastly what steps can be taken in the future to help it more. History across the key stages will be studied since it is essential to build on the child's previous learning if there is to be true progression.

First, what the meaning of progression is in the learning of history has to be defined. What we expect pupils to progress in obviously affects what we evaluate in their learning experiences. We need to work out whether this might be simply acquiring more knowledge, or a deepening understanding of historical concepts, both specific (like Reformation) and broader (like change and continuity); or coping with evidence at increasingly sophisticated levels or understanding how history is constructed. Such questions have long been at the heart of the history debate and the answer given here can be seen in the thoughts on what history is about in the preceding chapter.

It was in 1960 that Jerome Bruner first hypothesized that 'any subject can be taught effectively in some intellectually honest form to any child at any stage of development' and that if we wanted pupils to be mentally excited, to generalise from or organise what they have learnt and to remember it, we needed to make clear how the specific topics or skills fitted into the context of the broader fundamental structures of a field of knowledge (Bruner, 1960). In history this naturally led to the question 'What do historians do?'. The reply might be that overwhelmingly historians are people who get so interested in a historical topic or individual that they want to know more about them and so ask questions which lead them to further evidence and they keep refining their ideas, questions and understanding until they feel the need to communicate to others. For pupils to have some experience and gather some understanding of this they must be given the opportunity to enquire and investigate at their own level and to expand their understanding and skills as they progress through school. The underlying basis must be motivation through interest and excitement about people and events, what happened and why, which can be developed into real understanding through the skills and knowledge which are steadily built up by teachers assured in their craft and their own understanding of history and how it is constructed. Progression will be seen in:

- expanding knowledge and understanding of the past;
- increasing understanding of historical terminology and concepts;
- growing ability to use an increasing number of more complex sources, both primary and secondary, and to see how and why people interpret history in different ways;
- improving investigative, organisational and communication skills.

Progression thence should be measured in how far pupils will be able to formulate their own questions and answer on their own at a sophisticated level without structured help. As Bruner (1960) and De Bono (1994) have said, imagination and creative thinking need to be stimulated and developed, not put in any strait-jacket.

Having considered what, hopefully, children **could** learn from history, it is necessary to work out what might reasonably be expected from them during different moments in their cognitive and affective development and how they could be helped to progress from one level of skill and understanding to another.

Research on children's learning in history

In the past, history in the primary years was often neglected whilst in the secondary years it was often dictated by the type of learning required for O level, then GCSE (and even, at times, A level). It is certainly wise when thinking of progression to think first of what is the ultimate aim, but it is also important in pedagogical terms to be aware of what children of different abilities and needs might reasonably be expected to do and understand at any given age and to build up from that stage. The National Curriculum predicated 'planned progression, through increasing demands on pupils' knowledge, understanding and skills' (DES, 1990a). The inference from this is that those involved in the teaching of any subject know how to develop this in pupils but the reality is that we are not so sure how children learn and progress in history. The paucity of evidence on this is well rehearsed (Cooper, 1992) although much has been constructed on the work of researchers such as Booth, Schemilt, Ashby, Lee, Dickinson and Cooper, the focus of which was mainly on the limitations of R. N. Hallam's work (Culpin, 1994). Research into the teaching of history has been increasingly empirically based and where this has used a wide range of age and ability, as in Peter Knight's two pilot studies on testing children's understanding of people in the past, it has been able to make clearer to teachers what they can reasonably expect from pupils. The Schools History Project also helped build up a bank of knowledge on what secondary pupils could achieve in history. The various research mentioned has shown that:

- quite young children can begin to develop an understanding of the thoughts and feelings of people in the past and historical concepts and of how to investigate historical problems and make hypotheses on evidence;
- historical content does affect the level of children's responses (as most teachers know from experience);
- children only gradually come to expect people in the past to be rational, intelligible beings and their explanation of actions is limited by their own insufficient knowledge of the world (Ashby and Lee, 1987; Booth, 1987; Cooper, 1992, 1994; Dickinson and Lee, 1984; Knight, 1989; Schools Council, 1976; Shemilt, 1980, 1987).

There is, however, little research directly on **progression** in children's historical skills and thinking, although those studies which show how children make sense of historical concepts imply how such thinking may be developed. Chris Sansom has effectively used such work, particularly Shemilt's, to illustrate how development of the concepts of change, cause, development and motive as well as the idea and use of evidence may be achieved through a process-led curriculum (Sansom, 1987). In the CHATA project Alaric Dickinson and Peter Lee are building on previous research to investigate how pupils' ideas of historical enquiry and explanation progress between the ages of 7 and 14 so that teachers and publishers can address such ideas and influence them (Dickinson and Lee, 1994). As will be seen, the implementation of the National Curriculum has stimulated much thinking on progression although there is a need for much greater use to be made of case studies.

Progression and the National Curriculum to 1995

Much of the rationale for progression in history in the late 1980s onwards has been developed from HMI's *History in the Primary and Secondary Years* of 1985, the clearest empirical guide of its time to what may be expected from children of different ages in various historical skills and understandings. It was one of the key documents used by the History Working Group in the production of their *Final Report,* although other British, Irish and European evidence was used also (DES, 1985, 1990a). The principles of Bruner too were influential as could be seen in the use of the inter-twining cone and helix (Figure 2.1) which represented pupils' simultaneous progression in historical knowledge, understanding, conceptual sophistication and in performing historical tasks. From the twin helix were devised four (later reduced to three) attainment targets, each of which had ten levels of progression or statements of attainment (Bruner, 1960; DES, 1990a). All subsequent modifications of National Curriculum history have been based on this.

Are the attainment targets, therefore, what pupils should be working towards in history? According to Ian Colwill (1992) they 'define what all good history teaching is about – knowing and understanding what the past was like, understanding why and how things happened, and appreciating how we know about the past'. Certainly the writers of the 'new history' developed from the 1970s would agree that such must be the core of good school history (for example, Rogers, 1984, 1987). As seen above, research has shown that primary and secondary children are capable of learning like this especially if they are encouraged by skilful teachers to participate in open-ended investigations and discussions in a course specifically focusing on historical concepts (Cooper, 1994; Sansom, 1987). The previous chapter argued that this is the type of history to be encouraged together with a growing sense of balance, depth and significance and a deepening grasp of history's uncertainties and complexities.

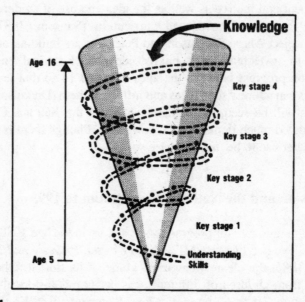

Figure 2.1

In the original Order, however, initially the relationships between the attainment targets tended to be either missed or confused. The worst example was probably the way attainment target 2 and attainment target 3 were simply lumped together although they were quite distinct, albeit related to each other through their links both to primary and secondary sources respectively and to the different strands of attainment target 1. Concentration on the statements of attainment deflected learning down a path of disconnected skills and concepts. Not having enquiry and communication as an attainment target was crucial since the whole emphasis on doing history becomes different if they are under-valued. Asking key questions is the bed-rock of sound historical enquiry and as Alan Kelly says the identification of these is of 'crucial importance …because it leads to an understanding that historical "facts" are inert until activated by a question' (Kelly, 1992). Progression should reflect an increasing ability to select, explain, plan and communicate history and draw inferences from it.

Although, therefore, the attainment targets rest on that broader interpretation of history in schools which had developed since the 1970s and which is adhered to here, the statements of attainment on which assessment and therefore, in all likelihood, planning and teaching, were to rest, had no research foundation. Rather than anyone ever having demonstrated that learning in history progressed this way, these levels were imposed upon the working group by a remit which insisted on adherence to the Task Group on Assessment and Testing's recommendations (DES, 1990a). The statements of attainment were *not* progressive, for progression in history is neither linear nor capable of being compartmentalised into little boxes or statements, but they appeared to be so, especially as the Non-Statutory Guidance said that the 'abilities represented by the statements of attainment are placed across the ten levels in the order in which they are likely to be learned' (NCC, 1991a). They were not levels of response as in GCSE which at least were very much based on what pupils had answered or were likely to answer (Culpin, 1994). The statements of attainment were helpful guides to which skills and concepts of their attainment target should be covered but for some considerable time this was hardly the aspect stressed. It was 1993 before INSET resources from the NCC, for example, emphasised that the statements of attainment were 'not...hurdles which require discrete tasks but broad indicators for planning' with skills in 'lower level' statements of attainment needing to be constantly refined and developed in more 'challenging contexts' (NCC, 1993, a, b, c).

The problems of teaching to such an artificial construct as the statements of attainment and these being bound up with assessment, and therefore progression, indeed proved to be a major stumbling block in National Curriculum history as was foreseen by many from the beginning (Dickinson, 1991; Grosvenor and Watts, 1993; Watts, 1992). Teachers either knew that they were being asked to fulfil requirements which did not match their experience of how children learn history or they viewed the statements of attainment in isolation without considering the amount of knowledge, the difficulty of the activities, or the context in which the tasks are done, relative to the level of attainment. Even more than the lack of time to get through the syllabus, the statements of attainment encouraged mechanistic teaching and a tick-box mentality with little impetus towards holistic history and no links drawn either between topics or key stages (Grosvenor and Watts, 1993; Watts, 1992). But pupils' understanding and skills **are** affected by particular content, context, teaching and learning methods and styles as OFSTED recognised (OFSTED, 1993a). Working towards an invalid hierarchy of technical competences and producing endless short answers to atomistic tasks actually prevented pupils drawing together their knowledge and understanding and investigating history properly.

The problems of teaching to the statements of attainment in a meaningful way were exacerbated by lack of time to teach the huge amount of content and the complications of assessment which accrued before Standard Assessment Tasks were temporarily disallowed for history. These further prevented teachers from looking beyond the attainment targets and/or the content to the rest of the programme of study (Brace, 1994; Phillips, 1993; Watts, 1993). Yet the attainment targets and programme of study, including both general requirements and study units, needed to be permanently intertwined. Putting them together made sense of the Order; for example, attainment target 1c – understanding of different ideas and attitudes of people in historical situations – fitted naturally with looking at different perspectives in history and social, cultural, religious and gender diversity.

The very difficulties of the first years of the National Curriculum in history nevertheless engendered much thinking and action research which clarified and extended understanding of pupils' thinking and progression. There was much advice on planning, for example, a vital factor meeting pupils' needs and ensuring progress (for example, McAleavy, 1994; NCC, 1991a); on how to teach meaningfully to the attainment targets and what a level might mean (Colwill, 1992,); on grouping the level related criteria statements of attainment of the attainment targets in a more meaningful and coherent way so that they more obviously showed progression (for example, Kelly, 1992). The latter was done especially by grouping levels around pivotal ideas which could be used as broad aids for planning and constantly reused in different and/or more challenging contexts. In Carol White's discussion on progression she focused on general good teaching methods such as asking more challenging questions, using more difficult and wider ranging sources and drawing on a wider and deeper framework of knowledge as well as making such activities explicit within the framework of the history attainment targets (Lomas, 1993; Shephard, 1993; White, 1993).

NCC INSET resources for each key stage expanded on the theme of how to help pupils demonstrate their levels of knowledge, understanding and skills as laid down in the statements of attainment through their use of the content in the programme of study (NCC, 1993b, c). So did other teaching resources such as the Schools History Project journal for history teachers, *Discoveries*. Certainly in any key stage many questions asked in history cannot be satisfactorily answered without exploring content in some depth. The helix of knowledge in the National Curriculum asked not just for more history but, rightly, for greater understanding of it too. Knowledge, understanding and skills should progress together and the NSG grids proved an important way forward in planning so that this should happen (NCC, 1991a) but there were difficulties. This was not because knowledge was not considered important and those who have made much public noise suggesting that teachers would do otherwise than base their pupils' learning on a bed-rock of knowledge were merely demonstrating their own lack of understanding. Teachers readily affirm that content and skills go together: if either is likely to be neglected by a teacher it is rarely content. The problems were far more to do with how to teach in any depth or coherence in the time available the amount of knowledge apparently expected and how to do this in relation to the understanding and skills delineated in the attainment targets. As Peter Lee has argued, 'An overloaded, overspecified history curriculum taught by overstretched teachers is a recipe for disaster'. It would be better to have a framework of knowledge which can be 'gradually elaborated and differentiated', an 'open', 'usable' structure capable of meeting the government's criteria of continuity and progression and giving pupils some understanding of the discipline itself (Lee, 1991).

To help pupils progress, objectives, tasks and learning outcomes needed to be tied up more. Assessment needed to be an integral part of this to 'measure what is important in terms of pupils' learning in history, not make what is easily measurable important' (Dickinson, 1991). The years 1990-94 have seen much advancement in the understanding of how to do this particularly in Key Stage 3. The very problems of teaching National Curriculum history generated NCC, CCW, SHP, SEAC, OFSTED work on progression (*see also Discoveries*, 1993; Harper, 1993; McAleavy, 1993; Scott, 1994). In fact, although the National Curriculum was pushed through before enough relevant research had been done, the results of its first years of operation, in themselves, can provide empirical data vital for better teaching in the future.

Teachers themselves have provided such data as the following two local case studies illustrate. At Derby Moor School, Derby in 1993, through Ann Whitlock's *Leonardo Project,* liaison was made with a feeder school whose year 6 were studying Egyptian history. Derby Moor's drama GCSE class were set up to teach them on this having redesigned their studio as Tutankhamun's tomb. The exciting resulting project included enquiry and communication in each key stage, finding and selection of sources, links across the curriculum (science, maths, music etc. were all included), language development, finding out how historians discover history, serendipity. All this was done with multi-ethnic pupils, both girls and boys, of different ages and abilities (Whitlock, 1994).

In Redditch near Birmingham, Barbara Parkes explored with a year 2 class the history of a timbered, thatched house in the middle of the modern housing estate around the school. Using a mixture of local sources, the 1891 census and pictorial material of all kinds, she led the children through a series of varied and interesting activities which were both carefully structured and allowed each pupil to explore and communicate at their own level. Change over time, fact and opinion, understanding different people in the past were some of the concepts developed in the sequence of activities which ended in a Christmas visit to the Victorian schoolroom and parlour of Hartlebury County Museum. Such activities at such an early age can lay the basis for increasing sophistication in historical enquiry. An attempt at a previous school, however, to extend similar work across the key stages had foundered because the middle school 'did not have time' to follow such work up and even suggested that the infant school should not start it.

Both these examples demonstrate what can be achieved with young children and then developed by imaginative teachers planning within the structure and framework of National Curriculum history. Certainly an emphasis on what pupils can do in school history should lead to a more holistic view of how children can develop their ability of 'how to work in the history way' (Fines, 1994).

Finally, valuable work has appeared on differentiation, a necessary part of progression and brought to the fore by using the statements of attainment, although hardly a new issue (*see* Gosden and Sylvester, 1968). Colin Shephard, for example, reminded teachers that differentiation is that 'process of helping individual pupils to improve their historical knowledge, understanding and skills as rapidly as they can' which has always been at the heart of successful classroom teaching. He stipulated that the following are necessary for pupils to make good progress:

● to have clear objectives which the pupils understand;
● to set up schemes of work through which the objectives can be achieved;
● to maintain constant formative assessment by written comments or discussion;
● to give pupils the opportunity to revisit skills and concepts through solving similar problems in different contexts;
● to build on what pupils have already achieved;
● to motivate pupils by a range of styles and methods;
● to use open-ended tasks and encourage pupils to take risks.

Shephard rightly stressed that in any lesson how pupils are grouped, how the teachers and resources are deployed, whether the work is differentiated by outcome, input, question or task must relate to the central concern of involving **all** pupils in worthwhile historical activities. Very importantly, Shephard argued that progression is necessary not just in the attainment targets and statements of attainment but also in knowledge (including perspectives, diversity of societies, experiences of men and women) concepts and historical enquiry. His list for identifying areas for progression is a clear, common-sense way of tackling preparation for the classroom (Shephard, 1994):

• coping with increased amounts of information, more complex events and materials, less familiar events, longer periods, a range of types of source material, less structured work, independent work;
• increasing ability to be relevant and precise, to select, recognise the tentative nature of conclusions, ask questions, generalise and to produce extended writing.

The 1995 Order

On progression, therefore, as has been demonstrated above, much work has been done on what is feasible and what was not and on how to tie up knowledge, understanding and skills. At the same time, there was little on how progression either in the use of knowledge, for example on British history, social and cultural diversity, the experiences of men and women or, to some extent, in enquiry and communication, takes place. Nor was progression across the key stages much considered. These issues will be investigated in other chapters of this book. It is clear, however, that the investment of teachers, advisers, ITT tutors, writers and NCC officers was considerable and much greater sense made of the Order for history as a result. Such 'enormous' investment was officially recognised by Sir Ron Dearing who hoped to wean out 'complexity, over-elaboration, over-prescription and excessive content' from the National Curriculum (Dearing, 1994). In SCAA's extensive consultation for the review its officers emphasised that an effective model in history should demonstrate clear progression within and between key stages but without giving the impression that progression is rigidly linear. It was also important to allow for progression without performance being 'capped'.

Has the new Order helped clarify progression? There has certainly been a very conscious effort to make it do so as can be seen in the very presentation itself. In each key stage there is a key focus statement with defined content and Key Elements neatly and clearly set out on a two-page spread. This makes it much easier than formerly to grasp the interrelationship of the component parts whilst the wording of the latter attempts to clarify the necessary progress in knowledge, understanding and skills between the key stages. Such a presentation is all the more important since the programme of study now contains all the knowledge, understanding and skills to be taught and assessed, the Key Elements including the essence of the former attainment targets. The one all-embracing attainment target is at the end of the Order to be used only for summary judgements particularly at the end of the key stages. Its level descriptions relate closely to the Key Elements.

The focus statements are intended not only to 'provide a focus for teaching and learning across the key stage' but also to 'identify the ways in which pupils' knowledge, understanding and skills are expected to develop in each key stage' (SCAA, 1994c). Subtle wording can be seen to denote progress. For example, from Key Stage 1 to Key Stage 3 children should move from setting 'their study of the past in a chronological framework' to being helped to 'develop a chronological framework by making links across the different study units' (DFE, 1995). In Key Stage 3 there is nothing on chronology in the focus statement although there is in the Key Elements. In the new Order the key stage statements focus not only on content but also link knowledge and skills, for example, in Key Stage 3 asking for pupils to be given 'opportunities to use their historical knowledge to evaluate and use sources of information, and to construct narratives, descriptions and explanations of historical events and developments' (DES, 1991; DFE, 1995). The above directive on communication in Key Stage 3 is not foreshadowed in the Key Stage 2 focus, however – a discrepancy which does not help links across the key stages. Similarly, only the Key Stage 3 focus mentions different perspectives of history.

There is now a much more obvious effort to indicate how pupils may progress in the very content of history:

'The content studied progresses in depth and range across the key stages. Pupils move from a focus in changes in their own lives, to those of people around them to those in a time beyond living memory. Study of famous personalities and events develops into studies of particular times, periods and societies.' (SCAA, 1994c)

This does not mean that the type of history experienced in the earlier years cannot be studied later. Learning about 'the lives of different kinds of famous men and women', for example, in Key Stage 1 is developed by the requirement in Key Stage 2 'Life in Tudor times' to look at some 'major...personalities' and in Key Stage 3 'Britain 1750-circa 1900' and 'The twentieth-century world' to gain both an overview and to study in depth 'main...personalities'. Biographical material can, of course, be introduced into the syllabus at any time. Focusing on personalities is nearly always a stimulating avenue into history and one perhaps somewhat lost in the first years of the National Curriculum. Doing it at recurrent intervals over the key stages should mean that by the teenage years it can be done with increasing complexity and depth.

This presupposes, of course, liaison across the key stages. Links across the key stages, especially in building up concepts, need to be stressed to help progression. Although there is less revisiting of the same material than formerly, there is constant reference to the same issues, for example, the power of the monarchy. The requirements to study aspects of the different countries of the United Kingdom, Britain in its European and world context and history from a variety of perspectives appear in each programme of study. They are placed with content rather than the Key Elements where progression is spelt out but can, with careful planning, enable a steady build-up of understanding of the complexity of these issues.

Greater complexity and depth are in fact integral to progress here and made more possible since both content and prescription have been reduced. Extra time and greater opportunity for teachers to exercise their professional judgement as to what is best suited for **their** pupils should enable that greater depth of study which allows proper investigation, enquiry and meaningful communication and, thus, progression in real understanding and the skills of doing history. This is, of course, provided that the time allocated to history is not correspondingly reduced and a vicious downward spiral continued, resulting in history being a marginal subject.

In Key Stage 2 study unit 1 and Key Stage 3 study units 3 and 4 greater depth is actually written into the units and could/should be into others, for example, Key Stage 3 study unit 2 'The making of the United Kingdom...'. There is more flexibility and choice so teachers can help pupils progress in understanding of a particular issue as they think best suits their pupils. It might be, for instance, that one class could be led through a key stage steadily building up its understanding of women in history throughout; another class might do an in-depth study on this in one study unit and then pick up on it briefly elsewhere. All the study units are equally weighted now so teachers could use units 5 or 6 in either Key Stage 2 or 3 to concentrate in depth on a particular issue, for example religious differences in a community which perhaps can draw on previous work and certainly look forward to the future. Studying population change in a local community in Key Stage 2 or the black peoples of the Americas in Key Stage 3, for example, could equally develop pupils' understanding about the complexity of the features and diversity of societies. Such choices are very important in linking Key Stage 3 and GCSE and the progression of pupils' learning in each as are those on what to study in depth in study units 3 and 4 of Key Stage 3 on the nineteenth and twentieth centuries.

The Key Elements 'characterise areas of progression in pupils' historical knowledge, understanding and skills' (SCAA, 1994c). They have become the everyday focus for planning, assessment and learning, thus, hopefully, removing the impulse to tick off boxes or base most lessons on a single level of attainment. Here above all can be seen what is intended by progression in the Order, not least in the way the Key Elements are so clearly set out on one page in each programme of study. The language of history instead of the shorthand referencing of attainment targets and statements of attainment delineates the five components of the Key Elements – chronological knowledge and understanding, range and depth of historical knowledge and understanding, awareness and understanding of interpretations of history, knowledge and understanding of the processes of historical enquiry and organisational and communication skills in history. Each appears in each key stage but with significant changes to reflect the likely variations in attainment. For instance, pupils should be helped to develop from being able 'to recognise why' things happened in Key Stage 1 to being able to 'describe and identify' in Key Stage 2 and to 'describe, analyse and explain' [authors' emphasis] in Key Stage 3. The same phrases may appear in more than one key stage, for example, 'characteristic features' and 'the experiences of men and women', in both Key Stages 2 and 3, but it is only in the latter that pupils are expected to 'analyse' these.

On the whole, indeed, the terminology suggests increasing understanding and independence of action on the part of the pupil. The move from finding out about the past and asking and answering questions about the past in Key Stage 1, for instance, to investigating 'independently' and asking and answering 'significant questions' in Key Stage 3 indicates a huge step forward which is unlikely to take place without planned and repeated practice.

Other changes should also help children to progress. Enquiry and communication – requirements in both the old and new Orders – are thankfully much more emphasised in the latter and thus hopefully will be in the classroom too. Although the only detailed progression delineated in communication is on written work, communicating 'in a variety of ways' (Key Stages 1 and 2) and 'using a range of techniques' (Key Stage 3) can be boldly interpreted by the teacher eager to utilise oral and visual methods both to suit the abilities of their pupils and to allow them to develop an increasing sophistication in this sphere. Historical enquiry now subsumes the use of sources – a connection much more reflective of actual historical practice than the old attainment target 3 and so should enable pupils to develop their understanding rather better. Tasks about bias and value, targeted on brief sources only studied for this purpose, have been off-putting for both pupil and teacher alike. Constant use of appropriate source materials as part of the process of investigation and finding out should more readily, even naturally with practice, lead to questions about reliability and usefulness. Within enquiries in depth, it should be increasingly possible to use longer and more difficult documents, if pupils' abilities to use these are nurtured. The references to sources in the new Order, if rather briefer, are nevertheless easier to understand and more realistic in their expectations than in the old. References to interpretation are less clear and it would be exceedingly difficult for a teacher who had not struggled with the statements of attainment of attainment target 2, albeit these were obtuse enough at first, to know what were the varying elements of this or how any progression in understanding might be made.

The principal features of progression, therefore, are now in the Key Elements of the programme of study. There is an attainment target – one instead of three – but its statements of attainment have been replaced by level descriptions to be used *not* for teaching, learning and everyday assessment objectives, but as a best-fit report on performance at particular points such as the end of each Key Stage. These level descriptions explicitly relate to and reflect the Key Elements. For example, in Key Stage 2 'range and depth of historical knowledge and understanding' refers to making 'links...both within and across periods', terminology which is reflected in level descriptions 4 and 5. On sources there is the same emphasis on the use of them within an enquiry and gradual building up from 'find[ing] answers to questions...from sources...' to using them critically, as there is in the Key Elements – a further welcome incentive to drop some of the dire, repetitive, boring and predictable exercises being offered on this before. Unfortunately, the references to progress in communication are even more exclusively on writing in the descriptions than they were Key Elements. Whereas it is welcome to include a progression through the beginnings of structured work in level 4 to 'well-structured narratives, descriptions and explanations' in level 7, the impression is a return to the arid accounts of the past. The excitement, interest and joy of doing history must be left to the imaginative expertise of the teacher.

In some cases there is deliberately little actual progression expressed, for example, 'demonstrate factual knowledge', and 'structured work' are phrases which can be interpreted at many levels. Since the level descriptions are 'best-fit' it is recognised that pupils have varying strengths and weaknesses and that progress cannot always be defined exactly. They also recognise tentative achievements; for example 'beginning to' is used often in levels 1 to 7. The greater clarity over what might be typical of any level and the more everyday language should aid teachers in their assessment of pupils.

For the first time levels 6 and above are explicitly tied to Key Stage 3 in recognition of the fact that the skills described in these must be linked to increasing depth and breadth of knowledge. The removal of levels 9 and 10 and the specific delineation of level 8 'for very able pupils' and the description above it for 'exceptional performance' are a welcome departure from the somewhat unrealistic expectations of 1991 in some quarters. Understanding the levels most likely to be attained in a year or over a key stage can help long-term planning as well as evaluation of progress. This is not to suggest trying to tease out level statements from the descriptions but rather to get an overview of the various interrelated skills and understanding which a pupil should be encouraged to work towards in order to move on from one level to another.

The driving force for planning and assessment is intended to be the Key Elements. Through these teachers can choose which content, concepts, issues, skills and methods of learning are most suitable to help progression in those areas. Having planned tasks with these objectives in mind, the pupils' work can be assessed accordingly. How exactly classroom work is assessed will vary from school to school but it would seem imperative that both pupils have some idea of what they are working towards and that, at least occasionally, they receive detailed oral or written comments on their progression. From the assessment of different pieces (and hopefully, types) of work, the teacher should be able at the end of the key stage to pick which level description best fits each pupil. An examination might be deemed helpful but coursework, at however simple a level, would better show how far pupils are capable of conducting historical enquiries on their own. Coursework is also better for demonstrating sustained achievement and subtleties of progress as well as building up skills necessary for GCSE.

It is worth noting too that in stressing the pupils' progression in knowledge of where and how to obtain further information, ask questions, formulate hypotheses and infer from evidence, a presupposition of active learning is implied. This stress on enquiry is a very different one from a given, learnt, handed-down history which would keep pupils very much as passive recipients most of the time. The opportunity could have been taken perhaps to break away altogether from the original attainment targets in the way, for example, that John Fines and Jon Nichol are attempting in the Nuffield Primary History Project (Fines, 1994) but besides the fact that such projects are in their infancy, Dearing explicitly banned introduction of new material and decided that, in the timescale available to him, it was best to modify the ten-level scale than abandon it (Dearing, 1994).

The question remains how far the replacement of statements of attainment by level descriptions are an improvement. In seeking to ease the difficulties of an untenable linear order, has much of the challenge as well as many of the subtleties and clarity on the objectives of history in schools disappeared too (compare, for example, White, 1993)? The terminology used in the level descriptors is certainly vaguer on what were attainment targets 2 and 3, although this might be a more realistic approach (but can they use sources 'critically' by level 6?). Unless guidance is given, however, it is unlikely that non-specialist teachers of history especially will either notice or understand the references to interpretations of history which is central, as argued earlier, to pupil entitlement.

Thus the huge amount of action research referred to earlier in this chapter must not be ignored for, despite constant reference to the now obsolete statements of attainment, much of this vital development work is still very relevant. It might prove indeed, that those who have developed themselves in trying to apply the National Curriculum and who have grappled with the attainment targets and their statements of attainment, will be in a better position to develop pupils' understanding of the Key Elements in the future than those who have ignored it or who come new to the National Curriculum in the next few years. This would be a telling effect of the early National Curriculum. Thus if the statements of attainment, when not in any particular order, proved to be a good guide to teachers on what could be accomplished in pupils' progress in history, they should be used as guidance in future.

Guidance on the new Order, indeed, will be all-important despite Sir Ron Dearing's strictures on not sending out any more masses of paper. Materials used by SCAA in the 1994 consultation exercises (SCAA, 1994 a–i) have already proved very useful to advisers and teacher educators and the promise of further exemplification materials is pleasing, particularly on assessment and the relationship of level descriptions and the Key Elements. Whilst the greater freedom for the professional judgements of teachers is to be welcomed, the latter need to have some idea of how to meet national standards. In Key Stages 1 and 2 they need to be able to prepare pupils for progression into the next key stage and in secondary schools for GCSE.

What is intended at GCSE is very important for progression. SCAA has explicitly aimed for continuity and the terminology of the latest proposals for GCSE criteria have moved markedly closer to that of the National Curriculum. The Key Elements are reflected in GCSE: in particular, understanding of how historical interpretations differ is an assessment objective whilst each syllabus has to look at history both from a variety of perspectives and at the 'social, cultural, religious and ethnic diversity

of the societies studied and the experiences of men and women in [them]'
(SCAA, 1994m). These syllabus directives are not spelt out so explicitly
in the other parts of the document but, nevertheless, they are there. The
grade criteria are in line with the level descriptions – a necessary overlap
showing progression into GCSE-type work.

Some paths forward

The 1995 Order will probably remain contentious for some time to come
until the new version of National Curriculum history is firmly embedded
in approaches to teaching and learning. Problems over progression can be
obviated by building on the mass of research already done and by
adhering to the following principles:

- progression relates to concepts, skills, language, the use of sources and
  content;
- each pupil must be given opportunities to:
- show what they can do;
- increase their understanding of historical terminology and concepts
  especially by revisiting these within and across the Key Stages;
- study the different perspectives of history and the diversity of human
  experience within an increasingly deeper and wider framework of
  knowledge;
- use more complex sources, both primary and secondary;
- recognise how and why people interpret history in different ways;
- have space and time to investigate at their own level with increasing
  independence;
- ask questions, return to these in different contexts and learn gradually
  to formulate hypotheses;
- try different ways of communicating their findings and in an
  increasingly sophisticated way;
- be engaged in an active and challenging learning process which
  stimulates interest and enquiry and therefore naturally leads into the
  understanding and skills which are part of history;
- experience teaching which has clear objectives, a variety of both
  methods and classroom organisation and is well and imaginatively
  planned;
- have regular positive and informative feedback on how they are
  progressing and how to progress further.

These principles of progression are generic across the continuum from
five to sixteen, not only across Key Stage 1 to 3 but also into GCSE and

beyond. They need to be planned for carefully across the key stages, within them and for individual study units. This can be done by utilising a grid (such as in Figure 2.2) which can be used for planning within a study unit or key stage or across key stages. It is for the teacher to decide how often opportunities for each aspect should be given or revisited within each key stage. Such grids can also be passed on to the next teacher to aid efficient planning. This is as important within a school as liaising with the next school in the pupil's career.

Year/Unit		Revisiting
Key Issues/questions		
Terminology and Concepts		
Perspectives		
Diversity of society including gender		
Representation of the past/interpretations		
Enquiry, investigations and use of sources		
Communication		

Figure 2.2

In these ways progression to 16 and, indeed beyond, is possible for those taking history. Tasks may be set directly on any aspect or be generic. Setting good historical questions which can stimulate investigative skills and call on a range of responses to promote individual progression in varying skills and understandings is one way in which progression on a number of fronts can take place. Certainly, as stated earlier, the best method of stimulating progress at any stage is to involve children in exciting, engaging history. This was at least the intention of the original *Final Report* (DES, 1990a) as of some Key Stage 4 and A level projects which have had to be abandoned (for example Fines and Nichol, 1994). But progress, certainly in all the areas described above, will not just take place by some kind of osmosis; it has to be planned.

Resources and progression

Finally, much planning has necessarily been based on the resources available. How far they have allowed for progression is, therefore, very important. The new books for the National Curriculum made great play of attending to progression but some, although colourful and visually exciting, contributed much to bitty exercises and a two-page spread on every topic approach which militated against holistic history and demanded too much from too little. They often did not cater for progression either through or across key stages or for differentiation or mixed abilities. Many of the problems accrued from the speed at which the National Curriculum was implemented, forcing authors to be the interpreters of the Order without time to pilot or trial their materials. For the future there is need for more interesting narrative, more on individual people and cultural contexts, more stories, longer and more challenging sources with more contextual information, greater opportunities for studies in depth and, perhaps above all, an attention to appropriate language. Pupils of all ages and abilities can navigate all these if they are taught to do so and encouraged to express themselves in a variety of ways suitable to their needs and capacities (Fines, 1994; SCAA, 1994l). 'Are books now allowing more for progression?' is an important question and should be applied also to GCSE books.

There is also the question of resources for and the training/education of teachers, helping them to plan, understand children's thinking and progress and how to evaluate for progression. In 1991 there certainly was much prescription without true reflection. More is now left to teacher expertise and professionalism and with the experience of the last 4 years it should be possible to make progression a firmer objective and plan for it better. Continued research is needed on how children learn history especially using the huge amount of action research which is in effect being done all over the country. Whatever the national requirements there must be space for questions to be asked as agendas change. Teachers must be helped to keep up with the latest research both in history itself and the teaching of it (for example, SCAA, 1994l). But there is more to history than this. There is a need for breadth and depth of understanding rather than detail and it is in this that pupils must progress.

3

Ensuring progression through effective liaison across the Key Stages

Sue Bardwell

With the introduction of National Curriculum history in September 1991 came the expectation that, at last, a basis for continuity and progression between different phases of education had been established for pupils aged 5 to 16. Teachers of history had high hopes that now they had a framework which could provide opportunities for developing clear links across schools with different aged pupils. Indeed, the History Working Group claimed in its 1990 proposals to the Secretary of State that one of its aims was 'to improve continuity in the study of history between primary and secondary schools' (DES, 1990a). So it is both disappointing and disconcerting to find that OFSTED's 1993 report on the second year of implementation of National Curriculum history states, 'With a few notable exceptions, contacts between schools serving different age ranges remained limited and there had been little discussion between schools about standards and progression in history' (OFSTED, 1993a). Clearly, the History Working Group's aim is some distance away from being achieved. OFSTED's conclusion begs further consideration. What has gone wrong? What are the reasons behind this failure to realise the History Working Group's aim? Is it an attainable goal? Did the Statutory Order for History provide sufficient opportunities for teachers to achieve effective liaison? How realistic is it to expect greater links at this still early stage in the implementation of National Curriculum history and to make judgements on this issue? Or, on the other hand, should better progress have been made between schools in developing continuity in the study of history? Furthermore, will the Dearing changes assist or hinder liaison developments?

This chapter seeks not only to explore these questions and some of the underlying difficulties involved in liaison but also to offer some ways forward for the future. Firstly, how justified is OFSTED in drawing attention to the low level of effective liaison in history between schools? In many ways, it is hard to refute the need for collaboration. Most teachers of history would agree that for pupils' progress to be appropriately planned, consideration must be given to pupils' prior learning and achievements. Effective teaching must use the assessment of pupils' progress to inform teachers' future planning. Given that the English and Welsh system of education has breaks in pupils' educational experience by introducing transfer to a different school, albeit at different ages throughout the country, there has to be some kind of liaison between the different phase schools. So if there is a general consensus about the need for ensuring continuity and insufficient systems are in place to achieve this, OFSTED is right to point out the deficiency.

But of course, it is much easier said than done. The organisation of education into different phase schools immediately produces structural difficulties in establishing continuity, compounded by the recent legislation which permits parents and pupils to select a school of their own choice. There are now many secondary schools receiving pupils from over 20 different primary schools, and there are many primary schools whose pupils choose to transfer to a variety of secondary schools. There is also a significant diversity of choice between first, middle and upper schools. Whilst they desire collaboration, teachers rightly question the kind of effective liaison in such circumstances with so many schools and teachers possibly being involved. Yet even where there are more regular transfer patterns and close proximity of schools, liaison has still been difficult. In many instances, the changes in schools' personnel can act as a barrier. Links are established between individual teachers from different phase schools, but do not continue to flourish when teachers move or roles change.

Time is also important. In many primary schools – junior, infant and combined junior and infant – the role of history co-ordinator is not always given a high priority compared with other subjects, and the co-ordinator is not often given sufficient time to carry out effective liaison. Enthusiastic co-ordinators are often frustrated by this as are heads of secondary school departments. On the other hand, attending joint meetings after school on a regular basis is difficult to sustain with all the other demands on teachers' time. Furthermore, it is not always easy to identify and bring together all the relevant teachers to discuss pupils' progress in history, particularly those teachers who have classes at the transition point between key stages. For example, should there be liaison not only between the primary history co-ordinator and the secondary head of department but also between the Year 6 and Year 7 teachers? If the latter is desirable, how can the year 6 teachers find enough time to discuss history when similar demands will be made of other subjects – and where would history come on the priority list? Equally, how feasible is it for a secondary school to allow enough time for all Year 7 teachers to meet with the Year 6 teachers?

Another factor which has hindered progress in effective liaison is the failure to establish the purpose of collaboration. Again OFSTED's report points out, 'Even where contact was well established, there had often been little discussion of standards and progression in history' (OFSTED, 1993a). Too often the partnership between primary and secondary schools is imbalanced. Only occasionally does collaborative planning and a real sharing of teaching and learning strategies take place with teachers from both phases regarding each other as equals. Some primary schools have looked to secondary history teachers for advice and support in developing expertise and resources. Sometimes, primary schools even use secondary teachers to teach history lessons. Equally, some well intentioned secondary teachers approach primary colleagues with offers to 'help out' by supporting them in the classroom or teaching an aspect of a study unit. Secondary teachers tend to see themselves as the history experts, and only rarely does a primary teacher teach or support in a secondary classroom. All too often, the contribution of both partners in the process of collaboration is not fully appreciated. Sometimes, there is little understanding of the different approaches used by primary and secondary teachers and the nature of different curriculum organisation. Mixed-age classes and cyclical schemes of work are usually unfamiliar aspects of education for secondary teachers to come to terms with. At best these issues are additional difficulties which need to be overcome, but at worst they can cause clashes of ideology and personality and ruin any future liaison.

Even where there is frequent liaison between schools, the focus of collaboration is not usually sufficiently targeted on those issues which will assist in establishing continuity and progression – namely how children learn history and how to judge standards of achievement. Schools have justifiably concentrated on establishing history study units in their curriculum, finding the appropriate resources, coming to terms with the statements of attainment and developing assessment and recording techniques. It is hardly surprising, therefore, that progression between schools has not yet been fully tackled. Teachers have understandably been initially concerned with getting things right in their own school and only now, as the first cohort of children to have studied

National Curriculum history from the ages of 5 and 7 are moving through the system, is progression becoming a serious issue for many teachers.

In those parts of the country where transfer of pupils takes place from first to middle to upper schools, OFSTED has found that the extent of contact between teachers with responsibility for history is sometimes greater. This is largely due to the need to reach agreement between schools over the selection of study units. However, OFSTED also points out that whilst this has been successfully achieved in some areas, in others the resulting agreements are not always satisfactory nor are they always honoured. For some schools these agreements are an additional layer of prescription and teachers feel they do not always allow their children's needs to be met appropriately. On the other hand, where there is close collaboration between schools, effective planning strategies and common assessment activities have been developed. Unfortunately, OFSTED have found this to be the exception to normal practice. Indeed, even within some middle schools, there has been a struggle to establish both a progressive framework and a coherent view about the teaching of history across Key Stages 2 and 3, with an integrated topic based approach operating in Key Stage 2 and discrete history teaching in Key Stage 3. Sometimes this results in an introductory unit in Year 7 entitled 'What is History?', since the school does not feel the children have yet studied any 'real' history in Key Stage 2, even though they have followed National Curriculum history units, albeit in an integrated programme (OFSTED, 1993a). A further factor in making liaison problematic is the transfer of records between schools. Again, OFSTED's 1993 report comments on this issue, 'It was not yet common for records of pupils' attainment in history to be transferred with them' (OFSTED, 1993a).

Successful transfer documentation has long been a difficult objective to achieve. In terms of the National Curriculum, the various changes to assessment and, particularly for history, the reporting requirements have delayed effective developments in this area. Also in many feeder schools there is no clear view about what information should be transferred. Even where feeder schools have thoughtfully assembled details of pupils' achievements and accomplishments and passed these on to the receiving schools, it is rare to find this information being usefully deployed to plan pupils' future work. Often this is the result of poor communications within the receiving school which prevents teachers of history from obtaining access to the documentation. Sometimes, even if teachers receive the documentation they do not value it and pay it scant attention. Most worryingly, there is now a consequential perception in many teachers' minds that there is no point in expending valuable time on preparing transfer documentation because it will not be put to good use.

As ever, there are exceptions to the norm, where good systems of transfer documentation are developing. This usually involves teachers in careful profiling of pupils' progress in history over a period of time and dated, detailed recording of pupils' achievements and competences in relation to the statements of attainment. These records are then passed on to the pupils' next school and are used to inform planning and sometimes the grouping or setting of pupils. Sometimes, the transfer records are accompanied by examples of pupils' work and occasionally supplemented by discussions between teachers about pupils' achievements.

Thus far, this chapter has concentrated on teachers' and schools' role in effecting, or more frequently, not effecting liaison. But what did they have to work with? It is equally as important to examine the role of the original Order for National Curriculum history in this process. Its structures and content must surely shoulder some of the responsibility in placing barriers between schools? Firstly, although it prescribed a framework for historical study, it was still open to interpretation by schools and contained elements of content choice. Clearly, as the response to Sir Ron Dearing's initial consultation procedure showed, for many teachers, the choice was insufficient and the prescription too burdensome and rigid. Yet, even with this prescription, pupils' experiences of history vary as they are taught by different teachers often in different ways in different schools. Hence, it is hard to see how continuity could ever be established unless choice was sacrificed for greater rigidity. The Order's statements of attainment sought to provide a progressive learning approach to the study of history, but these have also been found wanting, being criticised for forcing teachers to use them in a strait-jacket fashion when planning and assessing pupils' work.

Furthermore, teachers and textbook writers interpreted statements of attainment differently and hence it was difficult to develop a real consensus about standards of achievement – even between teachers in the same school let alone between teachers from different schools. Nevertheless, many teachers were beginning to work hard at moderating assessments both within their own school and in cluster groups containing teachers of different phase schools, only to find their efforts frustrated by the arrival of the Dearing Interim Report in July 1993 with its proposals for a slimmed down history curriculum and changes in assessment. It is not, therefore, surprising that the valiant attempts of teachers to work with the statements of attainment were put on hold until the arrival of the revised history curriculum. Thus the original Order was not as helpful as it could have been in establishing a continuous and progressive framework for teaching and learning history. In trying to avoid over prescription and yet provide an entitlement of history for all pupils, the original history Order fell between two stools and missed its target. It has therefore been widely criticised – although actual teachers of history, many of whom appreciated the problems in trying to provide both flexibility and a minimum common base of history, given more time, may have made the Order work more effectively.

When it comes to considering the implementation of National Curriculum history, the role of in-service training and published materials needs to be analysed in terms of their contribution in facilitating effective school liaison. Much of the training and support documentation has been specific to a key stage, and more recently related to individual study in Key Stages 2 and 3. This is what teachers felt they needed to implement the new curriculum speedily and effectively. The same can be said for textbooks – publishers responded to teachers' needs by focusing on different topics associated with a specific key stage. For publishers and INSET providers, the flexibility for schools to time the teaching of units to suit age groups for their own choice at Key Stage 2 and, to a lesser extent, at Key Stage 3, means that building progression into their publications and training is very problematic – which age group should they address, what prior knowledge and understanding can it be assumed pupils will have? It is therefore not surprising that most materials published so far are specific to an historical period in isolation, with some trying to cover a range of statements of attainment. INSET tries to cope with progression issues by addressing a variety of ages and abilities when focusing on an individual study unit. Rarely, are there opportunities for Key Stage 2 and 3 teachers to attend jointly a training session which for example covers Roman Britain and the Roman Empire, or Tudor and Stuarts and 'The Making of the United Kingdom'. At Key Stage 1, where the content is less prescriptive, it has been easier for more attention be given to planning for progression by publishers and INSET providers. Yet even here, the number of published materials which build from Key Stage 1 to 2 are few and far between, as are those that provide a link from Key Stage 2 and 3.

On reflection, should INSET have placed more emphasis on progression within and across the key stages from the start? To be fair, many trainers did initially focus on whole-school planning, especially at primary level, but much of this involved the selection and sequencing of units, although good efforts were made by many schools to make coherent links between Key Stage 1 and 2. Generally, this has been much easier to organise in combined infant and junior schools, than in separate infant and junior schools, although successful collaboration is not confined solely to the combined schools. Mention has already been made of the variable effectiveness of such planning in those localities where there are three tier systems. But since the initial training, most INSET has tended to concentrate on increasing teachers' knowledge of different periods of history. The GEST courses for primary history are an example of this trend. It can be argued that if INSET had persisted with studying and exploiting those opportunities of continuity which existed in the original history Order, more teachers would have been more aware of the need to liaise across schools to plan for progression. In turn, this may have created more demand for schemes on progression from publishers.

However, it would be misleading to suggest that no INSET work has occurred nor published material produced to promote effective liaison. The 1993 NCC guidance materials began to tackle issues of continuity and progression and provided useful suggestions to help teachers plan their work accordingly. Furthermore, in many parts of the country, there were and are good examples of in-service training which brings teachers from different key stages together to look at pupils' work and to consider planning for progression and continuity. Some encouraging results have been achieved in primary schools where Key Stage 1 and 2 teachers have collaboratively produced progressive schemes of work based on grouping and targeting certain statements of attainment in different year groups. Yet even when this has been done, there are limited opportunities for co-ordinators to monitor practice and evaluate the effectiveness of the planning. In secondary schools, many schemes of work are being planned to address progression within Key Stage 3 and gradually more are beginning to take into account what the pupils have learnt in primary school. Interestingly, OFSTED points out in its 1993 report that the Year 7 introductory modules on historical skills, so prevalent in the past, are disappearing. However, OFSTED goes on to counter this by stressing that there is still scope for more work to be done on progression when it states: 'at Key Stage 2 and 3 the links between the various study units should be made clear to pupils' (OFSTED, 1993a). It would be both wrong and unfair to conclude that teachers have given no thought to the importance of liaison. There have been encouraging signs that more teachers are becoming increasingly aware of the kind of history being taught in different phase schools and the need to take account of this in schemes of work. Unfortunately, the arrival of the Dearing Review, its subsequent holding arrangements on assessment and the uncertainty surrounding the inevitable changes to National Curriculum history understandably created an hiatus in many teachers' thinking about how children learn history. Teachers justifiably believed that until they could be sure of the new ground rules for history, issues of progression and effective liaison could not be seriously addressed.

In Key Stage 4 history, the various changes to the original Order clearly illustrate how difficult it has been for teachers to plan effective liaison from Key Stage 3 to 4. At the outset of National Curriculum history, there was a mismatch between the Key Stage 3 programme of study and the existing GCSE syllabuses, both in terms of content and skills. Teachers were waiting and preparing for the implementation of the Key Stage 4 programme of study, which had been designed to build on the Key Stage 3 study units. This was compounded by delay in implementing the original Key Stage 4 programme and then the removal of compulsory history after 14. On top of this, new GCSE criteria were being developed on which new syllabuses should be based.

Faced with so much unknown territory, history departments found themselves in a dilemma – one which will last until 1996 when the new GCSE syllabuses commence. They could either change to a different existing GCSE syllabus which better complemented the Key Stage 3 programme of study, yet which could be altered in 1996 by the new criteria, or retain their GCSE course until the new syllabuses were devised. Both options contained problematic implications. Changing to a different existing syllabus may have provided better continuity with Key Stage 3, but would involve an outlay on expensive resources and an expenditure of time and effort in developing new schemes of work, which could be wasted when the new GCSE courses are introduced in 1996. By making no change, some aspects of Key Stage 3 work could be repeated after 14 and would possibly involve using old resources badly in need of replenishment or replacement. Generally, whilst feeling dissatisfied with this choice, schools have coped as best they can, some taking a gamble by altering their GCSE course, others trying to adapt Key Stage 3 to provide a better match with their existing GCSE. It is not unreasonable, therefore, to conclude that effective liaison between Key Stages 3 and 4 has not been assisted by the number of changes made at the national level to history's position in the post-14 curriculum.

This chapter has so far considered the value of liaison between teachers who share the education of the same children and deliberated on some of the problems confronting schools when trying to establish effective working relations with other schools and plan progressive schemes of work. It is now time to examine some ways forward. The advent of a revised history curriculum following the Dearing Review offers a chance to learn from past experiences and build on those developments which have been successful. However, in some ways, post-Dearing history has the potential for providing more problems for planning progression and continuity across the key stages. With regard to content, there is less prescription, more choice for schools about what is taught within study units and wider opportunities to interpret the Order. The abandonment of statements of attainment and the unlikeliness of external assessments, at least for the foreseeable future, places responsibility for assessing pupils' progress firmly in the hands of teachers. Schools will have much more control over the kind of history they will teach, the methods they will use and how they will judge standards. Furthermore, the delay in implementing statutory teacher assessment in Key Stages 1 and 2 until at least 1998 and in Key Stage 3 until 1997 may have the effect of undermining the importance of assessment in history. These factors will inevitably lead to a diversification in teaching history and hence the need for liaison will become even more imperative.

Another major outcome of the Dearing changes is the removal of compulsory history or geography at Key Stage 4. With the broadening of options after 14, it is possible, though not inevitable, that fewer pupils may choose history than was expected before Dearing. Consequently, many pupils may well spend twice as many years studying history at primary school than at a secondary. This emphasises how important it is when children transfer to secondary school that their experiences and achievements in the primary school are valued, developed and extended during Key Stage 3, hopefully to encourage further study after 14.

So, how can the revised Order be exploited to ensure continuity and progression? All schools will be reviewing their curriculum models and schemes of work to take account of the Dearing changes. In those localities where cluster or pyramid groups have developed a strong foundation of collaboration, joint planning and selection of study units can become priorities. With the benefit of current National Curriculum experiences, there is every possibility that a coherent history programme can be developed for pupils aged 5 to 14, transcending the stages of transfer. Teachers who are fortunate enough to be able to attend such groups can also work with colleagues from schools of both similar and different aged pupils to decide how to assess pupils' achievements and begin to develop a consensus on standards. Some excellent work has already been undertaken in this area, notably in Warwickshire, where Ann Moore has worked with a cluster of first, middle, and secondary (ages 12+) schools, to produce examples of pupils' work from different year groups mapping out lines of progression. By comparing achievements of pupils across the age and ability range, teachers were able to distinguish phases of learning, and trace pupils' development. Two examples are shown in Figure 3.1. The first piece (a) has been written by a Year 1 pupil and is one of the outcomes from work on a local canal. The second piece (b–d) is part of a Year 10 pupil's course-work on the same canal. A comparison between the two shows progression in several of the key elements of the revised Order and provides a good stimulus for teachers to consider the ways in which this kind of progression can be planned from Key Stage 1 to GSCE. This material has been disseminated throughout the LEA by a display in the authority's teacher centre and will form part of the county's in-service training programme to support schools in their work on continuity and progression. Those teachers who participated in this work felt they had been able to gain much more insight into children's understanding of history. Moreover, because the cluster group had a specific focus, the trust and partnership between the teachers developed so the co-operation extended to a high level of communication with both teachers and pupils visiting each others schools. Additionally, they now have much more confidence in each others' judgements and a greater level of agreement about standards.

There are other instances of similar interesting work elsewhere in the country, particularly looking at assembling portfolios of pupils' work to help teachers within the same school develop more understanding about what pupils can do to demonstrate achievement in history. These portfolios comprise a range of pupils' work including drawings, diagrams, photographs of 3D models and fieldwork activities, a variety of written pieces and teachers' comments about pupils' oral contributions, investigative skills and motivation.

Sometimes, pupils play a part in assembling the portfolio and assess their own achievements. In some areas such portfolios follow pupils when they transfer to their next school. Some schools award certificates of achievement to pupils for their work in history which are then included in their Record of Achievement (RoA). Some secondary departments take a great deal of time to discuss with individual pupils their progress in history and use the RoA as a vehicle for transmitting information about achievement to the pupil, his or her parents, his or her next teacher or lecturer and possible employer. But these practices are currently the exception rather then the norm. Hopefully, more transmission of records and collaborative work will be undertaken and expanded. However, with fewer advisory teachers for history to act as catalysts for such initiatives, the impetus for cooperation and development will need to come mainly from teachers themselves. Yet experience to date has shown how problematic arranging and attending the necessary meetings can be and how little time there is for such work. Moreover, with Grant Maintained schools sometimes excluded from LEA networks, and the diversity of transfer patterns, such desired collaboration may not ever become a widespread reality.

So what is the answer to achieving effective liaison if regular meetings and discussion groups are not a feasible proposition? A minimalist solution could lie in the exchange of good quality documentation. But

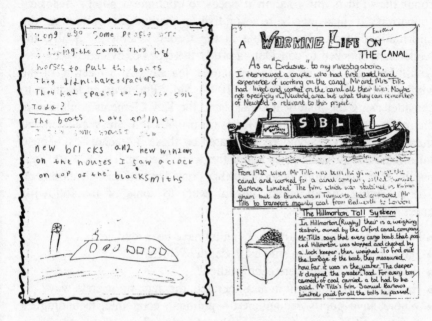

Figure 3.1a

Figure 3.1b

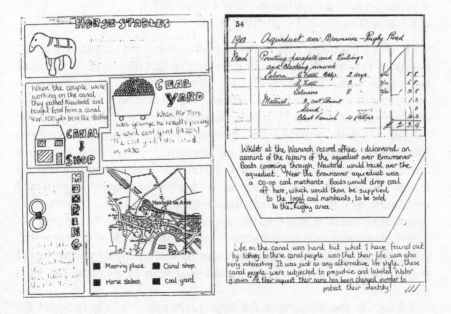

Figure 3.1c

Figure 3.1d

what does this entail? Clearly, the receiving school must be quite certain about the kind of information it needs to continue a pupil's historical education. It also needs to establish a method of collecting the information which is acceptable to the feeder school(s). Equally, the feeder schools need to consider carefully the types of evidence they feel would help plan the next stage of pupils' learning. At a meeting of the Midlands History Forum (October 1994), Sally Purkis urged teachers to consider using the historical content and the Key Elements contained in the revised history Order as the focus for progression. She suggested that links across schools could be facilitated by these if teachers exchanged information with each other about the work they undertook with their pupils. Her suggestions deserve further consideration and development. The receiving school could seek answers to some of the following questions:

- What historical topics (or study units) have been studied?
- Have any aspects been studied in depth? Which?
- In what school year were each studied?
- Has history been taught in an integrated, thematic or discrete way?
- Where have pupils encountered a political, economic, technological and scientific, social, religious, cultural and aesthetic perspective?
- What visits to historical sites/museums have been undertaken?
- What kind of sources have been studied?
- What kinds of interpretations have been used?
- What application of IT has there been?

The feeder schools could also be posing their own similarly focused questions for their main receiving schools so that they become aware of the way in which their pupils will continue to study history. Obviously, the questions would need to be tailored to specific school needs and, over time, be refined as more knowledge is acquired about partner schools and as other details need to be ascertained. For example, additional information could be exchanged in subsequent years about a school's approach to gender and diversity issues, its interpretation of British history as well as how the school is developing pupils' enquiry and communication skills. Such information should give a context to the level description which will eventually appear on pupils' reports, as 'best fit' descriptions may not be sufficiently accurate or detailed to help with progression. Ideally, such data could also be accompanied by portfolios of pupils' work in history which would also help to interpret the level descriptions.

Taking the list of questions a stage further and to help facilitate the exchange of information, appropriate retrieval forms could be devised to be completed by the partner schools. However, such forms would need to be created with care and a sensitivity to the work loads of the primary school teachers, and would be best introduced gradually over a period of time, seeking additional details to build up a good profile of what kind of historical experience a primary or first and middle school provides for its pupils. Clearly, such forms would also need trialling and mediating with partner schools, and where possible be devised collaboratively, but could be developed with a minimum amount of meeting time.

Above all, the receiving school will need to assure the feeder schools that profitable use will be made of the documentation. The time invested in supplying the information must be matched by the assimilation of it. For example, in a secondary school, all Year 7 teachers should have access to the documentation which details the kind of experiences their pupils have had and be able to value them in the classroom. It is important for pupils to feel confident and secure and so, for example, a teacher's recognition of and interest in, an earlier visit to an historical site can have a profound effect on a pupil's motivation. Additionally, patterns of learning and experience can be identified from the documentation and used to help formulate schemes of work which build on pupils' prior learning. News of pupils' progress in history should also be relayed to feeder schools, if only for example at the level of how many pupils opt to take GCSE history.

Such data collection and exchange are huge tasks to undertake and all the more daunting the larger the number of schools involved in transfers. Yet if such information is not available and utilised how can real progression be addressed? It has to be considered a sound time investment by both the feeder and receiver school, who must also see themselves as partners in contributing to the longevity of history as a subject on the school curriculum. Paper transactions are, of course, no substitute for personal contacts, but they are better than no liaison at all. Given the emphasis on the core subjects, history is not likely to figure high on schools' agendas for access to meeting time, INSET and resources, so a minimalist approach to liaison may be the reality for many teachers of history. Hopefully, all teachers of history can take the opportunity provided by the promise of a 5-year moratorium on curriculum change at least to develop effective and appropriate exchange of documentation. In so doing, it will be important to reflect on the experiences of National Curriculum history to date and build upon the lessons of the past.

4

Ensuring continuity and understanding through the teaching of British history

Paul Bracey

'Schools may also wish to look at how the curriculum develops pupils' sense of identity and their involvement in this country's common culture. There has been a renewed interest in ensuring that young people are "culturally literate", that they understand enough about their society and culture to take full part in it, feel a sense of continuity with the past and a sense of mission in carrying it forward into the future. The revised national curriculum addresses this issue, in laying down a statutory minimum in areas such as British history.' (Tate, 1994)

The current interest in cultural and national identity clearly relates to events in our contemporary world. Recent events in Eastern Europe illustrate the need to place such concerns in a historical context. Closer to home, issues of cultural and national identity are of paramount importance in discussions relating to Northern Ireland, the assembly movement in Scotland, 'race relations' and Britain's relationship with the European Union and the rest of the world. The different history curricula which emerged in Wales, Ireland and England together with the independent nature of the curriculum in Scotland reflect regional differences within Britain. However, it is also necessary for children to have an understanding of the development and perspectives of all people within these islands and their relations with the outside world. The purpose of this chapter is to look specifically at the teaching of history in England 5 to 16 in order to provide a framework for teaching British history in terms of a range of perspectives rather than a narrow interpretation of 'English history' which both distorts and misleads any attempt to understand our past.

To do this, the following chapter will consider the debate over the nature of British history and how this is reflected in the new Order. It will then outline five planning principles for realising a British dimension in the teaching of history 5 to 16.

The place of British history in the National Curriculum gave rise to considerable debate and controversy. To understand how this happened it is necessary to unravel the arguments behind this debate. At the time that John Patten was supporting a review of the National Curriculum, he stressed that to 'have national pride should be a virtue not a vice. That is why the Prime Minister and I are determined to see British history at the heart of history teaching' (Hennessy, 1994). He expanded on this when he requested that the draft Order be amended to include British history at Key Stage 1. However, some of the tabloids provided a very different impression, with headlines which screamed that key events in Britain's past would become optional (Bentham, 1994; Deans, 1994). Such views reflected the opinions of Chris McGovern, an outspoken right-wing critic of the National Curriculum, who saw British history in terms of 'great moments' and 'great figures'. Consequently, he felt that Henry V and Nelson were part of British history, but topics like the Vikings were not, since they were not an exclusively British experience! This amounted to studying the lives of the 'Great' but not of ordinary men and women, different cultural groups, or the wider spectrum of social, economic, or cultural history (McGovern, 1994).

To use the past to develop or promote a particular ideology is intellectually dishonest – a charge which can be put against any narrow definition of history as well as attempts to use the National Curriculum for explicit political objectives. Nevertheless, all historians are products of their age and it is therefore inevitable that contemporary issues will provide a catalyst for examining the past. This is not a problem, provided those studying history consider the personalities and events of the past in their own terms. The breadth provided by the Key Elements ensures that all areas, including political developments, get reasonable coverage which provides children with a holistic framework of the past.

McGovern's pre-occupation with specific personalities and events implies that patriotism and the transmission of a common identity should be the rationale for the selection of content. This becomes a particularly serious problem when content taught as British history is really 'English' history. This clearly acts as a smoke-screen over a real understanding of the diverse nature of British history. As Asa Briggs has observed there will, for example, be a difference between English and Irish attitudes to the Battle of the Boyne or English and Scottish attitudes to the Battle of

Bannockburn (Briggs, 1990). These differing perspectives will be at least partly explained by the different experiences which people from different regions and cultures have had in the past. While specific political events, such as the Acts of Union, may at first suggest the growth of a shared past, if sport, literature, religion, law and linguistic divisions are considered it can be seen that in many respects, regions have retained separate identities. Hugh Kearney has similarly argued that there is a need to recognise that Britain has a multi-national literature, a multi-national state and a multi-national history (Kearney, 1994). It follows that it is essential to place peoples' reactions to personalities and events in a cultural and geographical context. Neil Evans in a parallel debate with David Cannadine (Cannadine, 1987) over the nature of British history as taught and researched in Higher Education suggested that:

> 'British history needs to be constructed from the building blocks of regional and national boundaries within the British state. It needs to be fashioned from below [to] work up an understanding of the state...[This is] one way to construct it without Anglo-centric assumptions.' (Evans, 1988)

This perspective must also embrace the experiences of those migrants who have contributed to the development of a pluralist society in Britain today.

The balance between British, European and world history has been a second point of concern. The original Order devoted 50% of curriculum time to British history study units. The draft Order appeared even worse to Martin Roberts who complained it would lead to 75% of the Programme of Study being devoted to British history. This would be inappropriate, he argued, in a world where pupils' lives are particularly affected by world events (Roberts, 1994). Further, the Association for the Study of African, Caribbean and Asian Culture and History in Britain complained that the draft Order failed to consider the contribution to British society of peoples who are not of European descent (Blackburne, 1994). Clearly, the case for a more balanced syllabus was strong. Not only would the proportion of time given to non-British history affect pupils' perceptions of the world but the organisation of the Programme of Study into study units meant that scope for looking at different parts of the world at different times in the past was inhibited. The draft order also assumed that more time would be spent on the core units in Key Stages 2 and 3, which increased the bias towards British as opposed to European or world history (SCAA, 1994b). However, the final Order has improved this situation since it treats all of the study units equally (DFE, 1995). The assumption that teachers can go beyond the basic curriculum, either by extending or adding to the obligatory units, provides them with the chance to provide a more balanced syllabus. Whether this happens will of course depend both on the teachers of history themselves as well as the time allowed for the subject in the school timetable post-Dearing.

The new Order states that British history should, where appropriate, be set in a European and world context. This is a definite improvement on the vague notions of British history in the *Draft Proposals* (SCAA, 1994b) and reflects positively on the consultations carried out in 1994. This perspective is crucial if sense is to be made of events in Britain's past. There is no reason why British history should be inward looking. British history must encompass its relations with America, Europe and its empire, and its changing position in the world it encompasses. In this way it can be appreciated that not only has Britain influenced world events but has also been influenced by them. This shows that migrants from Europe and the rest of the world, together with the impact of other parts of the world on Britain and vice versa should be central to the study of school history. Rozina Visram developed this argument to make a particularly strong case for a black perspective in British history (Visram, 1994).

Finally, time and content overload was an area of contention in the original National Curriculum. As far as British history is concerned it could be argued that it is difficult enough to cover 'England's past' without taking on more topics. However, such an argument can be countered. First, many topics do not make sense without an appreciation of events in Britain as a whole. For example, pupils will gain a limited understanding of the outbreak of the English Civil War unless they develop a sound appreciation of events in Ireland and Scotland. Secondly, some topics, such as towns and agriculture, can be taught as easily from a British as an English perspective without any more time being required. Thirdly, all topics can be taught in varying levels of depth, including British history. This was seen, for example, in the approach used in the textbook *Societies in Change* which looked at general changes in Britain through maps and a chart before looking at Scotland in depth (Shephard *et al.*, 1993).

At this point it is appropriate to evaluate how the 1995 Order develops the idea of British history. The Areas of Study which frame each Key Stage state that Britain's past should be studied. At Key Stages 2 and 3 this includes reference to both Britain's role in the world together with Scottish, Irish, Welsh and English dimensions. Teachers at Key Stage 1 have the opportunity to look at different kinds of famous people and past events of different types, which should enable them to have a very broad interpretation of British history. The Key Elements relating to range and depth of historical understanding in Key Stages 2 and 3 require that social and ethnic diversity and links within and between periods should be considered. This provides a broad rationale for including multicultural and regional perspectives, as well as linking developments in Britain with other parts of the world.

In implementing these requirements, however, the Order offers very little detailed guidance. Focus statements for the study units provide little help and content details within them rarely provide support for developing an explicitly British, as opposed to an Anglo-centric perspective. At Key Stage 2 study unit 1, 'Romans, Anglo-Saxons and Vikings in Britain', states that pupils should be taught about 'the ways in which British society was shaped by different peoples' (DFE, 1995). However, this begs the question why the Celts are not included on an equal footing with the other groups. At the same time the specified content does not attempt to set the events in a wider European context. Study unit 2, 'Life in Tudor Times', has a more closely defined Anglo-centric focus on the Tudor monarchs and British expansion overseas. The break with Rome and expansion overseas provide opportunities for setting Britain in a European and world context. No attempt is made to suggest that teachers need to see the perspectives of people outside Britain and as it stands the content list could encourage a serious Anglo-centric bias. As for diversity in Britain the Armada, Raleigh and Essex provide opportunities for looking at Ireland, while topics on the Tudor monarchs and the Tudor way of life could also be put in a British rather than an English perspective; but this is not indicated in the document. Study units 3a, 'Victorian Britain' and 3b, 'Britain since 1930' state that pupils should be '...introduced to the lives of men, women and children at different levels of society in Britain' (DES, 1995). The Victorian unit does not provide any examples to illustrate how a British as opposed to an English perspective could be achieved, although more guidance appears in the twentieth century unit which states that the lives of people in different parts of Britain should be studied, as could immigration.

At Key Stage 3, study unit 1, 'Medieval Realms – Britain 1066 to 1500', relates to Britain in its focus statement when it says, pupils should be taught about some of the 'major features of Britain's medieval past including the development of the medieval monarchy and the ways of life of the peoples of the British Isles' (DFE, 1995). However, the content does not fully reflect this statement, since the title of the first half of the unit, 'The development of the English medieval monarchy' is alarmingly Anglo-centric with no attempt to focus on parallel political developments outside England. The only time aspects of the histories of Ireland, Wales and Scotland are mentioned is when they impinge on the history of England. Without being specific, the section on Medieval Society does have the potential to develop a British perspective, especially through elements relating to literature and language. Study unit 2, 'The Making of the United Kingdom: Crowns, Parliaments and Peoples 1500–1750' is supposed to introduce pupils to the '...major political, religious and social changes which shaped the history in Britain' (DFE, 1995). The content is an improvement on earlier versions of this unit in that there is scope to focus on relations between different parts of Britain rather than the Acts of Union. There is an opportunity to look at different regions, although this has not been made explicit. No attempt has been made to put events such as religious changes or the Glorious Revolution in a European context although the European study unit could be used for this purpose.

Study unit 3, 'Britain 1750 – circa 1900' is the first unit which specifically mentions Britain's role in the world when it says that pupils should be given an 'overview of some of the main events, personalities and developments in the period and, in particular, how worldwide expansion, industrialisation and political developments have combined to shape modern Britain'. The section on Britain's worldwide expansion includes studying the growth of trade and its impact on Britain and the colonies. Examples of suggested depth studies include relations between Ireland and Britain; the slave trade and its abolition and the development of Empire in an area such as India or Africa. The section on political developments refers to the effects of the American Revolution, the French Revolution and the Napoleonic Wars which could also be developed as depth studies. The focus statement, however, looks introspectively at Britain rather than its impact on the world (although this is contradicted in the section on Britain's worldwide expansion which refers to its impact on the colonies). There is no reference to different regions or ethnic groups within Britain, except for relations between England and Ireland within the list of suggested depth studies.

Study unit 4, 'The Twentieth Century World' provides some opportunity to look at Britain's changing role in the world, particularly with the break up of empires. Changing relations within Britain is indicated in the depth study – the partition of Ireland and its effects. However, the assembly movements, regional nationalism in Wales and Scotland and 'race relations' are not mentioned. Furthermore, it is difficult to see how major issues in British history can be fitted adequately into this vast unit.

This problem becomes particularly serious with the loss of history as a compulsory subject at Key Stage 4 where the *Final Report* (DES, 1990a) and original statutory Order (DES, 1991) provided an opportunity to consider such topics in detail. The draft proposals for GCSE (SCAA, 1994m) are vague since they only require that history is taught through a variety of scales such as local, national, European and non-European perspectives and that diversity within societies is studied where appropriate. Given that there will be different syllabi, much will depend on the examination boards' interpretation of the nature and place of British history and each history department's choice of syllabus.

It is clear that, as the analysis above shows, the new history National Curriculum provides an opportunity for a British rather than a narrow English perspective (DFE, 1995). However, as a means of structure and support it has a number of severe shortcomings. Firstly, it excludes the experiences of migrant groups between the Norman Conquest and the period after 1930, while regions outside England receive scant attention. Secondly, references to areas other than England in the British units are only made where they relate to England which re-enforces centralist Anglo-centric perceptions of Britain's past. Thirdly, Britain's relationship with the rest of Europe and the world is really only developed when it became a major power which re-enforces Anglo-centric attitudes. In preparing schemes of work and in our teaching it is clear that it is necessary for teachers to make full use of the European and world units and also to go beyond the National Curriculum to plan and teach a coherent history of Britain. What other help is available in official documentation?

More detail was provided in documentation which preceded the original National Curriculum (DES, 1991). *The Final Report* (DES, 1990a) certainly made specific references to various migrant groups in the 'Exemplary Information' sections (for example, Irish and Jewish migration in 'Victorian Britain'; black people in Britain in 'The Making of the United Kingdom'). Similarly, more examples were drawn from different parts of Britain (for example, distribution of wealth from land in England, Wales, Scotland and Ireland in 'The Making of the United Kingdom'; the Rebecca Riots and Newport Rising in 'Expansion, Trade and Industry'). However, Britain's changing role in the world was underplayed, as were the opportunities to develop Welsh, Scottish or Irish perspectives on issues within British history.

Nevertheless, the *Final Report* of the History Working Group (DES, 1990a) was helpful in providing a rationale for British history in sections 4.20–4.29 pages 16–18. This provided an idea of the scope of British history which corresponds with much of the analysis offered earlier in this chapter. This included an appreciation that relationships within Britain are complex and that while there have been moves towards political integration many aspects of Welsh and Scottish culture remain distinct. It pointed out that Ireland has sometimes been part of Britain in political terms and sometimes not. This idea was developed in support materials which were produced by the National Curriculum Council. For example, one exercise in *Teaching History at Key Stage 3* (NCC, 1993c) suggested ways of looking at how the United Kingdom became more or less integrated between 1500 and 1750. The Working Group also noted that migration from near and far could be used to explain the variety of cultures and languages in Britain and that major episodes, figures, and trends in English, Scottish and Irish history should be included in British history. They said that societies outside Britain should be studied in order to look at one's own country from a new perspective, as well as appreciate Britain's changing relations with Europe and the world. However, they failed to ensure that different dimensions of Britain's past should form a central part of work on British history, unless it was assumed that this naturally arose as part of what was then called Attainment Targets 1c and 2 on features of past societies and interpretations of history. What is also clear is that as teachers prepare for the future they should safeguard their access to past National Curriculum documentation.

On the basis of the above and the arguments which were examined at the beginning of this chapter the following five planning principles are given to assist teachers in developing a British dimension in their schemes of work:

- *The place of Britain should be seen in a European and world context.* This ensures that an appreciation of events in Britain's history are seen in their widest perspective.
- *Britain has always been an ethnically diverse society.* The range of the people who have made up British society at different times in the past should be studied. This ensures that the rich diversity of our cultural heritage is understood and that a distorted mono-cultural perception of our past does not prevail.
- *Regional diversity should be understood.* When looking at Scottish, Irish, Welsh and English dimensions to British history it is essential that the regions are looked at in the period before English domination to avoid an Anglo-centric perspective. Moves towards greater unity must be set against the ways in which regions retained separate identities.
- *Different interpretations of Britain's history should be studied.* Given that there is a debate over the place and nature of what constitutes British history it is appropriate that pupils should be given opportunities to look at different interpretations of Britain's past.
- *Different versions of events should be considered.* The relations between people in different parts of Britain and also between the British and people in other parts of the world must show each side's perspective.

The remainder of this chapter attempts to show how these principles can be achieved in Key Stages 1–3, given that this will be the only part of the 5–16 history curriculum that all pupils will experience. Key Stage 1 will be considered generally, but for Key Stages 2 and 3 the following units will be focused upon. 'Romans, Anglo-Saxons and Vikings in Britain' and 'Medieval Realms – Britain 1066 to 1500'. These units have been chosen, partly because the nature of their content provides a good opportunity for links and progression between Key Stages 2 and 3, and partly because these periods need a truly British perspective as a foundation for later units like 'The Making of the United Kingdom – Crowns, Parliaments and Peoples 1500 to 1750'.

The place of Britain in a European and world context

Britain can be set in a European or world context by looking directly for links with other people and places or by making comparisons with them. At Key Stage 1 pupils have to look at changes in their own lives and those of their families or adults around them. They also have to be taught about different types of past events. This could be achieved by looking at their own family histories and making comparisons with family histories in other parts of the world. The Development Education Centre in Birmingham has produced guidance on using a range of stories and approaches at Key Stage 1 in order to develop this sort of approach. (Cross *et al.*, 1994). Alternatively, Sylvia Collicot has shown how topics given for Key Stage 1, such as 'explorers', can be used to develop links from a local to a national and global context (Collicot, 1993).

At Key Stages 2 and 3 such links need to be developed in relation to the programme of study. Sallie Purkis provided a very positive outline of the scope of the 'Romans, Anglo-Saxons and Vikings in Britain' unit (which could equally be applied to the Medieval Realms unit in Key Stage 3) when she outlined its purpose as introducing children to aspects of human behaviour which relate to all people whether they live in the past or the present. She said it does this by opening up discussion about survival, motivation and migration. She also appreciated the value of teaching and learning processes in the classroom which operate beyond the subject matter in textbooks or the explicit list of content in study units when she said '...children will learn, as with most aspects of learning in primary schools, through activities such as...discussion: in particular, making comparisons with what is happening in our own world' (Purkis, 1991).

Pupils can be encouraged to compare events in Britain's history with what was happening in other parts of the world using a world timeline or by looking at evidence of what was happening elsewhere at a given time.

No current textbooks for either of the study units which were surveyed for this chapter deal with this fully, although some old textbooks (for example, Ha and Hallward, 1980) can serve this purpose. Putting illustrations in a wall display will help to develop this without taking up too much teaching and learning time from the topics which are being studied. British history can also be set in a wider context within topics. For example, Viking trade can show links between Britain, the rest of Europe and beyond. In the Medieval Realms unit at Key Stage 3 there are several opportunities where this can be developed. When looking at the role of the church, for instance, pupils can start by analysing the Mappa Mundi which clearly shows a British medieval perception of the world in both religious and geographical terms. Introducing pupils to evidence of the areas of the world which the map-maker[s] had never heard of provides a useful way of setting Britain into its global context. The children can then compare this with a map by Al Idrisi (illustrated in Shephard *et al.*, (1991) for example) which shows a Muslim perception of the world and discuss similarities and differences between them The pupils can then find out that some parts of the world were Christian while other religions spread elsewhere. Several textbooks show links with Europe or other parts of the world through topics such as language (for example, Aylett, 1991; Shephard *et al.*, 1991) and trade (Mason, 1991c).

Pupils can draw direct links between Britain and other parts of Europe when looking at the origins of different settlers. They will need maps to show where the people came from, why they left their homes and why they came to Britain. Most Key Stage 2 textbooks include maps showing where the Anglo-Saxons and Vikings came from, but generally fail to do this for the Romans (possibly because the Roman Empire was a compulsory part of the original Order for Key Stage 3). Reasons why the invaders left their homes are rarely explored although Farmer, for example, does include pictures explaining why the Anglo-Saxons and Vikings came to Britain (Farmer, 1991). Few books deal with the other parts of the world which invaders went to, a serious omission, if the invasion of Britain and settlement is to be put in perspective. Mason, however, showed that the Vikings went from Russia to North America (Mason, 1991b). Such gaps may be supplemented by some secondary school texts which were written for Year 7 prior to the National Curriculum, such as *The Vikings* by Jon Nichol which contained several maps showing the extent of the Viking's influence (Nichol, 1979).

This linkage can be developed in 'Medieval Realms – Britain 1066–1500' in Key Stage 3. The background to the Norman Conquest needs to be set in a European context and as an extension of the Saxon and Viking invasions. It gives pupils the opportunity to analyse Britain's place in the ambit of Europe, with its focus switching from north to south. Work on language, art, architecture, trade and conflict with France has a strong place in a British unit, and clearly shows the impact of Europe on its history.

Britain has always been an ethnically diverse society

The second planning principle relates to the diversity of peoples who have made and continue to make up British society. At Key Stage 1 this can be developed through work on the children's families. Pupils will be able to talk about relatives who have come from other places. They could find evidence of the person's birthplace and the reasons why they moved. When studying different kinds of men and women in the past, the experiences of black people such as Ignatius Sancho and Mary Seacole can be included. The Key Stage 2 and 3 units – 'Roman, Anglo-Saxon and Viking Britain' and 'Medieval Realms' – clearly provide an opportunity for looking at ethnic diversity. Sallie Purkis (1991) noted in her Key Stage 2 book that the invaders topic helped provide an understanding of our multicultural society. She also included tasks where pupils had to find out about immigration. It would certainly be helpful in drawing links between periods if pupils are made aware of other migrant groups who have come to Britain from earliest times to the present day. Some National Curriculum textbooks compared the Normans with the Saxons and Vikings. Farmer helped to put Roman migration to Britain into perspective by starting with a two page spread on the Celts before dealing with the Romans (Farmer, 1991). However, no textbook explicitly compared the experiences of these early migrants to those in other periods or in contemporary society. However, it is possible to use some pre-National Curriculum textbooks such as *The People Who Came: The History of a Multicultural Nation* (Page and Newman, 1985) or *Past into Present 3* (Fisher and Williams, 1989) to find appropriate information. Contemporary issues concerning racism can also be related to the treatment of the Jews in the Medieval Realms unit, which could be part of topic work on the church or relations between the king and people. For example, a chapter in *Contrasts and Connections* (Shephard *et al.*, 1991), provided opportunities not only to investigate the situation facing the Jews but the reasons why the situation developed and its results.

Regional diversity should be understood

The third planning principle, giving due attention to the Irish, Welsh, Scottish dimensions in British history, naturally relates to work on social and ethnic diversity and the growth of our multicultural society. However, it is appropriate to deal with that separately in order to consider fully its implications. At Key Stage 1 children's' work on family histories could be followed by plotting the places where people have come from on maps of Britain and the world. In classrooms where there is no obvious ethnic diversity amongst the children the idea of people moving can be used as a springboard for presenting them with case studies. Topics should include events and people from different parts of Britain, such as St. Columba. Indeed, the Key Stage 1 Standard Assessment Tasks materials appreciated a British perspective by including Welsh stories (SEAC, 1993). The units which are being looked for Key Stages 2 and 3 must give children a clear understanding that they are studying the whole of Britain. Whichever group out of the Romans, Saxons or Vikings is focused upon at Key Stage 2, it is necessary to consider their impact on Britain as a whole. This is partly because most areas were influenced by the invasions in some way even if they were not invaded themselves (Kearney, 1989). At the same time the fact that some areas were more affected by invaders than others helps to explain their different cultural identities. The most straightforward way of setting the invasions in a British context would be to distinguish the areas which were invaded and those which were not on a map of Britain. This is not always clearly shown in school textbooks and it is therefore a particularly useful class exercise for history, as well as having the added advantage of developing the children's geographical knowledge and skills.

'Medieval Realms' also needs to show how changes affected different parts of Britain as a whole. Unfortunately, several textbooks focus only on England's past. It is possible, however, to find appropriate information in some books. In his book on Medieval Realms James Mason included a chapter- 'England and the English: The kingdom of England and the British Isles' which, despite its unfortunate title, provides a brief political background to all parts of Britain in 1066, and repeats this overview later in the book (Mason, 1991c). Similarly, Ian Dawson and Paul Watson looked at the four regions of Britain through the use of maps (Dawson and Watson, 1991). Jon Nichol and Simon Mason briefly indicated how Wales and Scotland were ruled in the early Middle Ages (Mason, 1991c; Nichol, 1991). Tony McAleavy provided a clear background to the different areas in Britain in 1066 (McAleavy, 1991). Hence standard textbooks may be used to get a regional perspective of power structures and aspects of the economy and society.

Within this general framework it is necessary to use examples from different parts of Britain. Ideally, all topics – religion, towns, farming, etc. – would automatically do this. However, the reality is different and most examples are English based. Nevertheless, it is possible to give pupils exercises which draw information from different parts of textbooks to build up their own British framework. In 'Romans, Anglo-Saxons and Vikings in Britain' this has been done by most textbooks when looking at the spread of Christianity from Ireland to Iona and Northumbria. Sallie Purkis used a Viking stone found in London, but in her teachers' notes indicated this was just the best example in mainland Britain while others have been found on the Isle of Man, Orkneys, and Shetlands (Purkis, 1991). Mason included examples of objects found at Whithorn in Scotland and a Viking coin from Dublin together with a map showing both places (Mason, 1991b). Clearly, these examples are fragmentary and there is a need for the development of more resources such as a comparison between Dublin and Jorvik as Viking trading centres, for example. Similar issues are apparent when looking at resources for 'Medieval Realms'.

Some books certainly use maps which refer to all of Britain, although this is rarely supported in the text. Textbooks usually look at general topics in an English context and references to other regions are only dealt with, if at all, in chapters dealing exclusively with Scotland, Ireland or Wales. This encourages an Anglo-centric perception of British history. This can be partially overcome by getting the children to draw information from different chapters in the text when dealing with a topic. It is also possible to supplement general textbooks with specialised books such as *Wales in the Medieval World* (Broomfield, 1992). Finally, the standard textbooks may be supplemented with information from academic texts as shown in the following exercise on medieval farming.

An exercise which provides a British perspective to medieval farming:
What was farming like in different parts of medieval Britain?

We have looked at how people farmed in an Open Field Village. This was not the way people farmed everywhere. Sometimes this was affected by customs affecting the way they lived, or the type of land they farmed on. In the following tasks an * has been put against extension questions.

Task 1: Finding different types of farming taking place in medieval Britain

Look at the map in Figure 4.1, which shows farming in different regions of Britain.

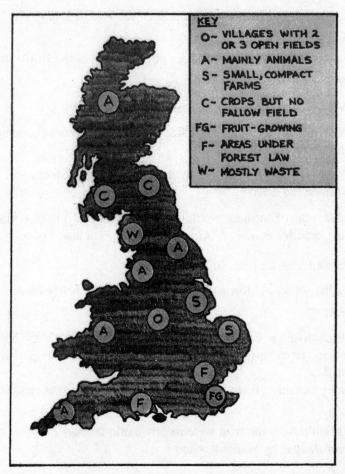

Figure 4.1 C. People farmed differently in different areas. Some areas did not have open fields. (In Aylett, J.F. (1991) *Medieval Realms*, p.17. Reproduced by permission of Hodder & Stoughton (Publishers) Ltd.

Write out the correct statements and correct the false statements in the sentences below:

1. Scotland was mainly open field farming.
2. Open field farming was mainly in the Midlands.
3. Animals were mainly farmed in the west of England, Scotland and Wales.
4. There were small compact farms in the east.
5. Which region has the map missed out?

Task 2: Matching the type of farming in medieval England to the weather and type of land

Look at the map in Figūre 4.1 and a physical map of the British Isles.

6. What type of farming took place in highlands?

7. What type of farming took place in lowlands?

8. What type of farming took place in the north and west (often colder and wetter areas)?

9. What type of farming took place in south and eastern areas (often warmer and drier)?

10. What sort of farming would you expect to find in the region you answered for number 5? Give reasons for your answers.

Task 3: What can we find out from sources?

Look at the sources below and answer the questions below them:

Source A:

'The Irish live on beasts only and live like beasts. They have not progressed from primitive habits of pastoral farming....Little is cultivated....'
Written by Gerald of Wales a supporter of the Norman invasion of Ireland.

Source B:
In the Middle Ages the Irish were mainly cattle-farmers.
Medieval Realms by Walter Robson

Source C:
...the analysis of pollen deposits...has thrown some light on agricultural matters...contrary to general belief – wheat growing was being cultivated in most of Tyrone through most of the middle ages...
K. N. Nicholls *Gaelic and Gaelicised Ireland in the Middle Ages*, p.114.

*11. Which source shows that its writer did not like the Irish? What makes you say this?

*12. Source A was written in the Middle Ages and sources B and C are recent textbooks. Which source do you trust the most? Give reasons for your answer.

*13. What letter or letters do you think a map of Medieval Ireland would need to show the type of farming there?

*14. Give reasons for any differences in the answers you gave for questions 10 and 13.

*15. What have you learnt about the difficulties in trying to find out how people lived in the past in this exercise?

There are different interpretations about events in Britain's past

The fourth planning principle relates to how Britain's history has been interpreted. At Key Stage 1 pupils can begin to interpret the past for themselves by finding out why people, both famous and familiar, did certain things, such as move to their locality in the first place. At Key Stage 2 they can begin to consider why some aspects of the past have been interpreted differently. For example, they can try to find out if the Vikings have been mainly seen as raiders and decide whether their trading and artistic achievements have been given due attention. Pupils can also be taught to focus on particular information and language in textbooks which shows the perception of the author. Not all books show a full British perspective as Farmer (1991) does in the following example: 'British people were now a mix of Celt, Roman, Anglo-Saxon and Viking'. It is also possible for textbooks to make misleading generalisations. For example the phrase 'For 300 years Britain was part of the Roman Empire' (Farmer, 1991) is too inclusive and does not indicate that large areas of Britain were not part of the Empire. Sometimes seemingly straightforward statements can lead to various interpretations. In the following paragraph, for example, possible bias for one group of people against another needs teasing out.

In the eighth century, Mercia was the strongest Anglo-Saxon kingdom. A Welsh monk wrote that Offa 'struck terror into all the kings and lands around him'. Offa was not friendly with the Welsh. Welsh raiders often stole cattle and slaves from Mercia. Offa attacked but failed to conquer Wales. Finally, Offa ordered a great dyke...(Farmer, 1991).

The issue of textbook bias becomes particularly significant in the 'Medieval Realms' unit. Pupils should be asked to find which chapters refer to areas outside England; where chapters on Ireland, Scotland and Wales are located and the language used to describe them. Negative perceptions can be seen in the following extracts:

'The peasants of Scotland were poor. They kept cattle and grew some oats and barley. They lived in earth shacks, which they shared with the animals...
In the Middle Ages the Irish were mainly cattle farmers. They used cows, not coins as money....' (Robson, 1991)

Both examples should be followed by questions about life in England, for example: 'Was the English peasant noticeably better off than people in other parts of Britain?' or 'What was the relative importance of money as opposed to bartering in rural England?' Pupils could also be provided with information which disagrees with the perception given in the textbooks.

When dealing with conflicts within Britain it is vital that the case for both sides is given. In the Key Stage 2 unit the perspective of the Britons against the Saxons needs to be given, for example. In the Key Stage 3 unit it is particularly important that conflicts between England and Scotland, Ireland and Wales look at each side's case. The most straightforward approach would be to help pupils to recognise bias in the selection used in texts, such as, 'Even before the Norman Conquest the rulers of England had trouble with their northern neighbours...' (Adams, 1991); 'Ireland was not yet safe. It was a problem which English rulers would have to face' (Aylett, 1991); 'English Kings could never feel really secure while the Welsh princes threatened the western borders and the Scottish king threatened the northern borders' (Shephard *et al.*, 1991). There need to be corresponding sentences illustrating how the Scots, Irish and Welsh felt on these issues.

If several textbooks are available it is possible to compare gaps and bias. In the case of the conflict between Llywelyn and Edward 1st, for example, most texts noted Llywelyn's refusal to pay homage to Edward but few looked at the reasons behind Llywelyn's decision from a Welsh perspective. Nichol (1991) and Robson (1991) are rare examples of writers who did do the latter.

Different versions of Britain's past should be considered

An alternative to looking for textbook bias when studying a conflict, such as between Llywelyn and Edward, is to look at their different versions of events. Both leader's arguments can be put on strips of paper. The children can then decide which ones would have been made by Llywelyn or Edward. Their conflict can be set in a wider context by making timelines of the histories of Wales and England, showing the rise of Gwynedd, the reasons why England encountered more invasions than Wales and the impact of Edward's conquest. (Useful information on the history of Wales can be found for example, in Allison and Brown, 1990.)

To summarise, the National Curriculum provides both an opportunity and an obligation to decide what we mean by British history. There is a desperate need to build up resources in this area, especially within general topics. Pressure of time, particularly with the loss of history's place as part of the compulsory curriculum at Key Stage 4 will make it difficult to do full justice to providing a British dimension up to and including the twentieth century. Where pupils continue with history beyond the age of 14 much will depend on the syllabus which is chosen. Nevertheless, within these constraints, current textbooks provide a start towards developing a British perspective as well as providing opportunities for pupils to examine how to set about interpreting Britain's past.

5

Ensuring continuity and understanding through the teaching of cultural diversity in History, 5–16

Peter Rogers

The new History document will provide the framework of history teaching for the next 5 years or so and is intended to take us into the new millennium. It provides a skeletal framework within which teachers should have considerably more scope than under the original document to design their own curriculum and to decide their own points of emphasis. It has created space for greater professionalism, but at the same time it has produced greater demands for this to be justified and the essential new requirement is for individual teachers, subject areas, or departments to produce a rationale for their history curriculum. This will have to be considered from a diverse range of approaches to ensure progression, development of historical knowledge and skills. The reduced document has avoided any requirements of pedagogy, leaving that to professional judgement within the framework of the Key Elements, which now constitute the basis for all planning, learning and assessment.

Within each programme of study, it is Key Element 2 which is specifically concerned with cultural diversity as an essential feature of the work to be undertaken. Given the skeletal nature of the current document in comparison with its predecessors, this is significant. Cultural diversity will have to become part of any school's rationale for history, but it will have to compete with the other factors which also need to be considered. This element of competition for emphasis is beneficial because cultural diversity has consistently constituted a contested arena within which awkward questions are asked about the values of society, the effectiveness of social democracy in Britain and the kind of history appropriate for a diverse nation facing the new millennium. Teaching to foster a sense of the reality of cultural diversity both in Britain and in a rapidly changing world will depend upon three things: the ethos of the school, the attitude of the subject co-ordinator and the commitment of the individual teacher. These constitute a descending order of hierarchy within the school and will determine choices of subject matter, decisions over curriculum balance and the allocation of scarce resources between competing areas of the school.

For a really effective approach there is no substitute for a school policy discussed at senior management level and endorsed by the governors of a school. Ideally it should actively embrace three key areas of equal opportunities: equality of opportunity itself or the assurance of high-quality provision for all; cultural development or support for different identities; and education for citizenship. By far the best guide for the formulation of a whole-school policy in these three interrelated areas is contained in the Runnymede Trust publication *Quality and Equality Assurance in the School Curriculum* (1992). It reintroduced a perspective that was lacking after an earlier decision of the National Curriculum Council not to issue formal guidance to schools on the multi-cultural dimension of the National Curriculum. This was criticised by the Trust's working party as implying to teachers, heads and governors that issues of racial equality, and justice in education are of little importance within the context of the Education Reform Act 1988.

The Trust working party made a useful and very thorough cull of the National Curriculum documents that emerged since 1988 which had purported to encourage cultural diversity and provided the official stance. In NCC *Guidance Document on the Whole Curriculum* it was stated that 'the whole curriculum' was 'much greater than the foundation subjects of the national curriculum' and included coverage of 'gender and multicultural issues' (NCC, 1990a). A year later, in a briefing paper, the NCC stated:

> 'Multicultural education is concerned with more than the needs of pupils from ethnic minority backgrounds. It seeks to prepare all pupils for life in a world where they will meet, live and work with people of different cultures, religions, languages and ethnic origins. Multicultural education is the professional responsibility of all teachers in all schools.' (NCC, 1991c)

These were high sentiments but constituted only a modest nod of the official head in a world where cultural diversity and inter-ethnic rivalries have become a dominant international theme since the ending of the Cold

War. More specific guidance had been given in NCC *Curriculum Guidance on Education for Citizenship* which stressed:

> 'the interdependence of individuals, groups and communities; ... Britain as a society made up of many cultures, ethnic groups, faiths and languages; the diversity of cultures in other societies; a study of human development and culture from different perspectives; international and global issues; the origins and effects of racial prejudice in British and other societies.' (NCC, 1990b)

These are consequently issues which one would expect to find within the history document, for there is no other curriculum subject in which cultural change constitutes the very bread and butter of the discipline.

The pruning knife has been taken to the original National Curriculum document and much else besides approaches towards cultural diversity has gone. Not only has the pedagogy has been stripped away, but the dissemination processes have spelled out that the new Order gives only the minimum statutory framework within which schools will be expected to make their own decisions on how to put the building blocks together. This is emphasised by the new parity between the various study units, with the former distinctions between core and supplementary study units now being removed. Choice of emphasis has become simultaneously more significant and at the same time it presents an opportunity to re-engage with old areas for new debate. All subjects will compete for part of the new space that has been created and necessarily also consider their rationales for curriculum content selection.

If the NCC has been short on advice and the current document is skeletal, the Runnymede Trust publication is bristling with sound ideas, some of which will be developed later in this chapter. It usefully brings together some of the varied features of cultural development and education for citizenship and emphasises the significant point that all children and adults have a wide range of loyalties, allegiances and identities, some of which are at variance with each other and all are in a continuous state of development. Equally important, personal identities occur within the context of uneven power and influence. These are issues which need discussion across the school community as a whole before considering their implications for each subject area. The discussion within the school as a whole is central. If it is simply assumed that individual areas will find their own level of involvement, then the questions raised will be pushed further down the school. When this happens it is more difficult for essential decisions to be taken, particularly on curriculum design and resources. Responsibility for the curriculum is now clearly vested in the governors but delegated to the teaching staff, and collectively they are answerable to outside agencies. All schools now live with one eye cast over their shoulder towards the next OFSTED inspection, when accountability towards parental aspiration will rank very high on the agenda. In the first instance, therefore, unless parents are taken into the confidence of the school where cultural diversity is concerned then the relevance to the curriculum will not be apparent. This can only be undertaken at the level of senior management of the school.

At the next tier down within a school the main onus for the balance of the history curriculum will fall upon the shoulders of the subject leader or co-ordinator. It will be their responsibility to provide the academic ethos of the subject and the rationale for the curriculum decisions that are taken. This is the point at which debate should become keen. A rationale which stresses cultural diversity goes, in the first instance, against the one of the main political thrusts of the document, namely the emphasis upon predominantly British history. It implies a willingness both to make study unit choices that create a diverse learning menu and a reading of British history which encompasses more than the great names and landmarks of our past. It means opting for an open-ended pattern of finding out and questioning that does not close off awkward answers. It also requires discussion among staff of the various ways in which they interpret the programmes of study. It demands a clear view of what cultural diversity can mean, how this can be built into policy documents on content, continuity and assessment and transferability between schools. Here again subject leaders will find the Runnymede Trust guidelines useful.

The Runnymede guidelines identify seven main points that include:

'the necessity to place all events within a wider world context, the different priorities and agendas which have produced different interpretations of the same events, appreciation of bias and the moral courage and decision making which have been part of struggles for justice and fairness in British history, and not least that migration movement and settlement are recurring themes in British and world history.' (Runnymede Trust, 1992)

The guidelines describe these as the basic history curriculum and they begin to identify the tension existing between competing approaches to British history and national image building through the history curriculum. A framework for the selection of study units also requires coming to terms with the knowledge-based approach to culture characteristic of the new document. It raises questions of the understanding of some central issues, discussion of which the subject leader or head of faculty should be instrumental in promoting. Cultural diversity is not an area with a simple practical approach capable of being bolted on like Lego. It requires understanding and permeation of the curriculum by some essential concepts, a global view of historical issues and a willingness to apply these ideas to the particular circumstances of a school. There is no blueprint, rather there are attitudes of mind which can inform the historical thinking of a department or year group of teachers. It is these attitudes of mind which will help teachers consider how the study units can be taught in such a way as to retain credibility within the statutory requirements, and at the same time produce alternative views of human experience in history.

There is an important initial point to be made: the new Order emphasises historical knowledge but knowledge about another person's culture has rarely proved a barrier to discrimination against them. Indeed, constantly re-emphasising the distinctiveness of a culture can be a means to justify differential treatment. It can reinforce the marginalisation of a person or group who do not share all the cultural assumptions of those who are the 'natural citizens' of the country. Within the history of multicultural education these ideas were effectively criticised from the early 1980s (for example, Miles, 1982). The knowledge base of the new document re-establishes it as an issue for the classroom practitioner. If the teaching about and analysis of cultural diversity is to be within the disciplinary bounds of history as a subject and to be knowledge based, then these areas of contention will need to be re-considered. This applies particularly to notions of culture, ethnicity and nationalism. The following are some questions that can contribute towards a possible agenda for history staff discussions:

1. What is meant by the term cultural diversity?
2. What problems are raised by it in an increasingly nationalistic world?
3. What is the British context?

They are far from exhaustive. Each of them has an extensive literature and there is no consensus of opinion upon them. It is their discussion that is as important as emerging with a correct answer. Where a department or individual members stand on these and related issues will determine the type of history and the values they seek to teach. It is assumed that whatever the position taken it will need to be justified to parents and governors. It will also need to pass the scrutiny of OFSTED, for the latter will in future be interested in the rationale developed by a department or area. The professional judgements made by subject teachers about the type of history they seek to teach and why, will now come under closer scrutiny as the range of professional choice becomes greater. In suggesting answers to these questions, what follows is a set of propositions rather than exhaustive surveys and they are intended to provoke as well as serve as a possible start for staff discussion.

What is meant by the term cultural diversity?

Cultural diversity is as much about power as anything else; it concerns class as well as 'race' and is the reverse of a mono-cultural society, if such a society has ever existed. Monoculturalism infers the sharing of language, religion, diet and economic activity to a remarkable degree. It would have to be a very simple society indeed, probably no more than a small band of nomadic gatherers and occasional hunters. Britain is clearly in a totally different historical category as it is an industrialised society with wide contrasts in wealth, life-style, and occupation and with clear regional distinctions of one kind or another. Above all it is a society with considerable differences in influence, power and status: all of which contribute to marked patterns of cultural diversity. These differences take expression in conflicting social and political priorities: tension, conflict and constant change are characteristic of industrialised societies and inevitably produce wide disparities in their outcomes for different groups communities and individuals.

Cultural diversity is historically embedded in any complex modern society. The influence wielded by particular cultures will depend on the wealth, prestige and power of those associated with it. It is the consequence of wide differences of political and economic influence; the more powerful a group the more influential their culture in the various forms it may take. The weaker a group the less significance is attached to their culture; it may be tolerated but it will have only a relatively weak status compared with a dominant group. The same applies to any human group or society. One important point to be borne in mind is that the non-European societies suggested for study units were exactly the same. They were no more homogenous entities than Britain, and should not be viewed solely through the lens of the dominant culture of the time. Imperial China, India from the Mogul Empire and Japan under the Shoguns were all highly stratified societies and need consideration in the round rather than through the limited lens of the dominant court cultures. Cultural diversity is more than a question of colour, religion, diet, music and other evidently 'cultural activities'. It is about processes that serve to differentiate human beings into groups with different access to power. Above all it is not biologically determined.

Problems raised by cultural diversity

Ethnicity is similarly not biologically inherited. At the 'common-sense' level cultural diversity is usually thought of in terms of ethnicity, but it is in fact a variant on the existing inequalities of a complex society and is a reflection of them. Ethnic groupings are self-protective voluntary alliances against the consequences of political and social weaknesses and they would be unnecessary in the absence of discriminatory experiences. Ethnic diversity is the most visible demonstration of a difference consciously maintained, almost as a challenge or statement to other groups. It is not a genetic phenomenon but is a chosen option, and it is usually a reaction against some form of group racialisation and collective discriminatory experience. Ethnicity uses a wide range of cultural baggage to justify itself and historic continuity is usually one of them. This is only a short step to an exclusive nationalism. The particular features of any given ethnic identity are less significant than the circumstances in which it thrives. The awkward conclusion is that ethnicity, like culture, is sustained by the over-arching control of a dominant group. Ethnicity is usually intolerant and its roots are to be found in deeply held, long-standing grievances that are capable both of historical selection and manipulation. The current ethnic mix in Britain is a reflection of past imperial links and trading patterns that are inextricably intertwined with British history. An understanding of this shared past is essential for a balanced view of the role of ethnicity in contemporary British society. On the international scene inflammable ethnic differences have re-emerged to fuel long submerged historical grievances and have produced a re-awakening of virulent nationalisms quite capable of dragging other nations into war.

Nationalism is a relatively recent phenomenon that dates from about the end of the eighteenth century; it deploys a selective ordering of the past and is a close relative of ethnicity. Since the ending of the Cold War the spectre of ethnically based conflict has once again begun to haunt Europe. It has produced in the name of ethnic purity, some of the most vicious fighting since the end of the Second World War. The question of nationalism, citizenship and civil rights raised by these events are central to consideration of cultural diversity at any level. It requires an accurate understanding of the nature of ethnicity. What has made the recent nationalisms in the former Yugoslavia so awful has been the particular notion of primary ethnicity. This argues that a person is born with their ethnic and national identity intact which is demonstrably incorrect and biologically impossible. Its most horrifying recent manifestation has been the so called 'ethnic cleansing' in Bosnia and Croatia, attended by systematic deportation, genocide and rape. The links between nationalism, ethnicity and right-wing movements are European-wide with each appealing to history to justify the current situation. It is occurring at the same time as older imagined identities are being challenged by new forces such as Europeanness. It is an area that cannot be swept under the carpet by choosing 'safe' study units, for sooner or later the question of 'Britishness' will arise. What is required is a profound understanding of how, in Benedict Anderson's useful notion, 'imagined communities' are sustained by selective treatment of the past (Anderson, 1983). The emphasis upon British history in the document inevitably creates a tension between the images of the British nation and those of cultural diversity.

What is the British context?

The British context is dominated by a number of linked questions, not least of which is the ways in which British culture has been seen as under threat from within. This has been portrayed as the consequence of the increased numbers of 'black' people within the country. Since the 1960's, 'black' people have been projected as a political problem of numbers to be controlled. The Labour party were shocked in 1964 by defeat in Smethwick at the hands of the overtly racist campaign of Peter Griffiths. As a consequence the overall consensus in British politics of both right and left has been to control 'black' immigration in a way that is selective and discriminatory. Black people have been presented as a threat to British social stability, with the problem being their presence rather than any inherent British xenophobia. Since that time no political party could hope to win votes by promising to remove immigration control. Despite Race Relations legislation, the legal position remains that 'black' people are historically and culturally outsiders whose numbers must remain a matter of government scrutiny. What we have witnessed over recent years has been the last throes of British imperialism. Those who came to settle and reunite their families in the UK were, by and large, historically part of the former empire.

One major consequence of these perceptions has been the assumption that with the completion of family reunion in the UK, the flow of migrants would almost dry up. Consequently the stabilisation of numbers, employment, social justice, education and other welfare issues became the main policy concerns. They focused on issues concerning integration, assimilation, discrimination and racism within a former imperial power. Immigration policy and social attitudes attempted to stabilise these migratory patterns. New forces, however, render this view of Britain increasingly anachronistic.

All governments are now finding that economic and political issues that could once be dealt with from the perceptions of national interest, have to be considered increasingly in collective forms. Miles has observed, '...the boundary of our economic and political field has been extended, necessitating an extension of the boundary of "imagined community" beyond that of each nation state in Europe'(Miles, 1993). These factors alone are sufficient in themselves to warrant a change of perception. To them must be added the global population movements of workers, refugees and asylum seekers that have dramatically increased since the 1980s and show every sign of increasing in the future. New factors have unleashed population movements of a scale larger than any seen for centuries. These will require wide-ranging international agreements on settlement and eligibility for citizenship. New patterns of spontaneous human movements have created an estimated 80 million migrants or people living permanently away from their counties of origin (Castles, 1993). Of this number approximately 15 million are asylum seekers; in addition 30 million are reckoned to be illegal in their status.

There is every indication that this phenomenon will increase rather than decrease with identification and response to it becoming increasingly more difficult. As industrialisation of less developed countries (LDCs) progresses, it will increase rather than decrease the flow of migrants as happened in the industrialisation of Britain. Yet simply to cope with their own population growth without the impact of modernisation, LDCs will need to create collectively an additional 36 million new jobs each year throughout the 1990s – an impossible task. What will increasingly emerge are 'push' factors which will generate further outward migrations. These will be occurring at the same time as traditional work patterns in the developed world are adapting to the restructuring of the global economy. The world has changed considerably since the original History Working Party began to deliberate upon the most appropriate ways in which to consider cultural diversity. They, alongside other policy makers, could safely assume that inward migration would no longer be a major issue, but that is clearly no longer true. Then there was the fall of the Berlin Wall.

During the time the initial History Working Party was meeting, the Cold War was accelerating towards an unexpected end and with it the end of the post-1945 world order. The simplifications of a bi-polar world, already eroded over the previous two decades, were crumbling and were replaced by new and uncharted international waters. Rather than the Cold War and an easy division of the world into East or West, free or oppressed, capitalist or communist, there has appeared a different landscape. This includes within its horizons, violent ethnic nationalisms, mass international migrations and the international *fatwa* on Salman Rushdie. The end of the Cold War marked a destabilisation of Eastern Europe and the fragmentation of political authority in the former USSR that released further population movements and ethnic conflict. It also highlighted another factor, the diminishing international role of the UK. While the

Cold War lasted, Britain had at least the luxury of redefining its post-imperial world role as the main, if only junior partner of the USA. Since the ending of the Cold War a reunited Germany has emerged as the dominant European power and increasingly the main partner for the USA. British national identity is now being re-forged in a world that demands more than the simplicities of the Whiggish interpretation of British history that pervades the history curriculum. The domestic debates about the cultural diversity of British society have been overtaken by a surprisingly unfamiliar outside world. They now need to accommodate the changed context within which children will be living during the twenty-first century.

These new international features would be more than enough to make a substantial rethink of the history document necessary. In addition the transnational forms of culture generated by satellite television and the constant growth of multinational conglomerates renders monocultural explanations of national identity increasingly inadequate. Britain cannot afford the luxury of attempting to isolate its schools from this broader world. They are asking them to protect a monocultural past viewed through a predominantly British historical lens by adopting the ostrich position. Those who shape the school curriculum have a major responsibility to create rather than obstruct an informed awareness of these new world forces.

Ideally all these issues need collective discussion by the teaching team under the leadership of the subject co-ordinator; this is relevant to all schools no matter what the age range. Television brings into the living-room, not just innocuous advertising, but also other powerful images. These constitute a daily experience for many children, particularly the images of war, so much of which is fuelled by ethnic conflict. Young children need explanations of what they see as well as 'Blue Peter' style humanitarian responses.

The subject co-ordinator takes an over-view of all that is taught within the school under the aegis of history. If their position towards cultural diversity is equivocal then the onus for devising alternative initiatives falls on the individual classroom teacher. This is clearly the weakest position of all as it demands the negotiation of much that would otherwise be taken for granted if there were effective school policies and a committed subject leader. The teacher in this position may feel vulnerable, always facing the necessity to justify the particular teaching approaches they are adopting towards any given study units. Individually they need to be sure of the implications of cultural diversity and how this can reasonably be reflected in their teaching. At the same time they need to be confident that they are delivering the curriculum to satisfy whatever critical criteria or performance indicators are brought to bear upon their work. The most useful way of approaching the task is by sustaining a view of history as a contested arena; given the balance of the document, a critical view of British history is central to this task.

The new document is minimalist and is sited on terrain marked out by the 'New Right', namely the need to reinforce the historical features of British culture. Hence the centrality of British history as a shared experience that bonded the nation together in a mono-cultural myth. This is a view of the world that requires challenge and an approach to history that is able to acknowledge alternative histories as a necessary component of the main body of the subject matter. British history is world history and the most intellectually reliable way to approach it is as world history.

It also means exploiting the latest history document for any given opportunity. Although it is shorn of pedagogic advice, the Key Elements of the current document are specific and the guidance of the earlier documents need not be discarded. The history Non-Statutory Guidance document was scattered with exhortations to ensure that the various study units were taught in ways which ensured consideration be given to cultural diversity; for example:

'Features of past situations should include the ideas beliefs and attitudes of people living in those societies, with pupils being enabled to see links between the histories of the British Isles and other parts of the world and an understanding of how events in British history can be seen from different perspectives....The cultural backgrounds of local communities should be reflected in the selection of the study units and cross curricular themes and should include consideration of citizenship....The various perspectives of any study unit should include social and religious, cultural and aesthetic approaches to any society.'

In addition pupils should develop what the history working group called 'the quality of open mindedness' which questions assumptions and demands evidence for points of view (NCC, 1991a). The initial recommendations were open to criticism for their assimilationist and cultural pluralist assumptions. None the less they had argued that something should be done to encourage such an open-mindedness and objectivity in the questioning of easy assumptions about British history and society.

The quality of open-mindedness will be determined, among other things, by the learning strategies adopted by any particular teacher, the nature of the ethos of their classroom and by the processes of assessment. Knowing the outcomes will determine the nature of the inputs. Cultural diversity has always encouraged open approaches and a teaching style which has respect for the individual learner and provided scope for difference of opinion. Even within the carefully structured study units of the National Curriculum there is scope for activity learning which encourages pupils to make connections, identify and expect differences to exist without taking a judgmental position. Support materials, artefacts, pottery, clothes, food, posters, postcards and museum visits can all provide tangible sources of evidence of cultural diversity being a norm rather than a deviation from a norm. If the assessment expectation is for pupils to detect and to understand these positive differences, then the teaching approaches will encourage it and the support materials reinforce it. Differences of opinion and discussion are essential skills within the educational process. Cultural diversity as a theme within the teaching of history can ensure that these features of education in the round are not submerged beneath the need to perform well in the local league tables. This is particularly true for Key Stages 2 and 3 where the emphasis upon knowledge can in the first instance appear too daunting to encompass an open-ended a teaching style.

This is not so in Key Stage 1. Here the emphasis upon knowledge is much less prescriptive but there is the requirement to be taught about changes in their own lives and those around them. This is the only part of the document where this emphasis occurs. It is very significant for two particular reasons: it values the child's own history and it values the child's own culture and that of their own immediate circle. What is being taught and remembered as history at Key Stage 1 is individual memory and from that is derived social memory of a personal and local kind. The child is valued, with obvious benefits for individual self-esteem and their history is taught, using familiar objects and artefacts. This will apply whether they have been brought up in a former Welsh mining village, an inner-city area or a leafy suburb. By the very nature of the individuality of the pupils, they will bring into the classroom a diversity reflecting their own and local circumstances.

There is a peculiarity here, because from Key Stage 2 onwards the memory activities will be profoundly different. Apart from learning about some famous people and some anniversaries, there is no real rationale for the manner of the transition. They move abruptly at 7 from individual and social memory at Key Stage 1 to the formal memory of the later study units. Within the Key Stage 2 units the significant features of knowledge have already been selected and signified. This is not the history that pupils will have experienced before the age of 7 and it is difficult to detect progression. The jump is not merely from small group memories to more sophisticated groups, but to 'national memories' which by-pass community, locality and gender altogether into a history of states. Only one further opportunity exists in the next 4 years to study the locality of the individual pupil through the local history study unit. This apart, they will be required to acquire, that is remember, particular forms of historical knowledge to demonstrate their progress in history when, in the first instance, they will have been introduced to it as an open-ended personal experience of remembering.

Many of the questions which have enlivened recent debates on how, at one level the past is selectively re-ordered, and on another the ways in which individual memory becomes social memory are encapsulated in this peculiar moment of transition (Furedi,1992). It is assumed that it is an unavoidable consequence of progression into more demanding forms of historical knowledge and understanding. There is, however, more to it than that; at its heart is the question of whose collective social memories and histories, and therefore whose culture, is being taught (Fentress and Wickham, 1992). The National Curriculum requires that the history taught in schools is predominantly British. The 'Right' have for long argued that one major purpose of history is to foster national cohesion and this is best served by a focus upon key events. Inevitably this will be the history of dominant or ruling élites. It is unlikely that sub-groups such as working class or peasant communities, trades unions and women's groups will share the assumptions by which the key events are selected. It can be argued that any National Curriculum history document will always be an exercise in deciding what is culturally significant in the national memory. That does not absolve it from providing an education that will equip children personally for the culturally diverse world in which they will be living.

For the subsequent study units effectively to produce progression, they will need to draw upon the experiences and concepts that have explained change in the lives of those around the children while at Key Stage 1. Unless this is done the relevance of the work will be lost. This progression is best expressed through Key Element 2. Throughout the document, this emphasises the experiences of men and women, cultural and ethnic diversity and links between local, British, European and world history. This clear commitment is carried over into the GCSE criteria, but is hampered by the balance of the National Curriculum document. The political parentage of the 1988 Act, has a particular view of the function of history in schools. The curriculum from Key Stage 2 onwards reflects this and is prefaced upon a relatively narrow and culturally limited range of content. It can be argued that there is opportunity to study non-European societies and indeed that the new skeletal document merely prescribes a minimum content which is not exclusive. In practical terms however this is not the case. The choice of 'A past non-European society' will be heavily dominated by Egypt at Key Stage 2 and it is highly unlikely that the Africanness of Egypt will find much mention in the process. Key Stage 3 is unhelpful because the suggested examples of non-European society are all highly centralised societies, which are not necessarily typical. Information and resourcing on them are not readily available without some degree of difficulty. This could well result in yet more schools emphasising the African slave trade with the consequence that the designation 'non-European', or 'non-white', will once again be caught in a conceptual trap of negative stereotypes. This influence will be perpetuated at GCSE. Without a broad grounding in appropriate non-European study units at earlier stages, schools and pupils are unlikely to opt for syllabi which, while interesting, are risky bets for producing the required grades.

What requires evaluation is the potential the current document has to promote among the young a world view capable of standing the test of time as they grow up into the twenty-first century. The world has not stood still since the process of curriculum review gained momentum in the late 1980s and the events of recent years would have overtaken any document. The international agenda has been recast to such an extent that the approaches to cultural diversity implicit in all the documentation that has appeared, including the latest, is now in need of significant revision. Cultural diversity can no longer be treated as if it were a purely domestic issue which will go away as assimilation takes its natural sway. New political alignments, massive international population movements and a diminished international role for the UK require a positive rather than an exclusionist approach to cultural differences. A state that is at ease with its own cultural diversity will be comfortable with international diversity.

Cultural diversity is a consequence of many factors and cannot usefully be studied historically unless it takes account of the political, educational and social explanations of it. Cultural diversity is not about understanding different cultures *per se*, although this can have its place. It is about the factors that give rise to difference at all levels in widely diverse societies and how history has treated these differences. It is as much about those histories which are not written as about those more powerful cultures which dominate our views of the past. At the same time it is about the fact that the past can be selectively constructed to justify the present. The central issue is power. However one chooses to define culture, the ultimate concern is the extent to which continued discrimination is allowed to blight life chances. It will occur to those defined as being culturally weak or as rank outsiders within our own society and are oppressed in others. Within schools it raises questions about individual behaviour, school policies and, on a broader canvas, equality of opportunity for all citizens in a democratic society. These ideas require space for reflective classroom activities on the part of teacher and pupil alike.

The success of individual schools in their approach will be influenced by where in the school hierarchy the issue is discussed. If left to individual teachers to create opportunity in their own way, it will be done without the support and encouragement of LEA policies and advice; as a consequence it could remain weak. At this level a clear understanding of the implications of the range and depth of historical knowledge and understanding contained in Key Element 2 is invaluable for the essential task of constructing a viable rationale. However, an effective blend of the greater levels of professionalism once again available to schools and an ethos that promotes equality of opportunity and outcome requires one significant element. It should be a matter for policy making at senior levels within the school.

6

Ensuring continuity and understanding through the teaching of gender issues in history 5–16

Erica Pounce

This chapter examines the development of women's history in the context of gender issues. It traces the gradually declining profile of gender issues through 10 years of government documents and examines how this has been reflected in resources, in post-14 courses and in implementation. It asks the question whether there is any evidence that women have finally been included in school history and whether there is any continuity within that experience. The chapter concludes that the strongest impetus for addressing equal opportunities issues now comes from OFSTED with the inspection process but that the flexibility within the new History Order leaves teachers free to take the initiative again in the teaching of gender issues.

Introduction

Since 1985, with the publication of *History In The Primary and Secondary Years: An HMI View*, government documents have pointed out the need to include women in school history. After 10 years, how much evidence is there that women have finally been included in school history and is there any continuity within that experience? Are the schools now offering a progressive learning experience about the roles of women in history? Do schools use early experiences involving listening to the memories of women, then build on with learning about individual women's lives? At secondary schools do they acknowledge womens' achievements in a wider context and then recognise why these have remained invisible for so long?

Gender issues in National Curriculum history

Perhaps the basic problem is that despite the rhetoric of National Curriculum history, the content, to a large extent, is reaffirming traditional white, middle-class, male English history, rather than challenging it. However, that verdict misjudges the foundations of National Curriculum history and gives little credence to the importance of the Key Elements and the general requirements and ignores the substance of the skills contained in the original attainment targets, especially in attainment target 2. Concern is based far more on the reality of National Curriculum history as it is implemented by busy teachers and interpreted by textbook writers who have used their energy in covering the content and have left gender and multicultural issues on the periphery. The coverage of gender issues in history still remains insubstantial, hazy, variable and is very far from being delivered in a coherent plan across the key stages.

In 1985 the DES report *History In The Primary And Secondary Years: An HMI View*, put women's history on the schools' agenda:

'...the lack of emphasis given to women in history syllabuses may have helped certain popular stereotypes to survive – that women have not been agents of change in history, for instance – and has the effect of giving pupils the message that our society attaches low status to female concerns...It is no longer acceptable to pay scant attention to women's lives in history. In the past, historians have been limited in their ability to write history because of the lack of sources available, or because the lives of women were not considered significant. Recent research, oral history and the reissuing of books written by women in the past, have made accessible some of the sources needed to give a more balanced view of women's role in history.' (DES, 1985)

Since this statement 10 years ago, an entitlement to learning about the experiences of women in history has remained implicit in National Curriculum and HMI statements. The tone, however, has, over time become increasingly more cautious in official documents. *History 5 to 16 Curriculum Matters 11* in December 1988 recommended that:

'history courses should ensure that women are not "invisible", that their changing social roles are made clear and that interpretations of the past which demean or obscure their experiences are avoided.' (DES, 1988)

The Final Report of the History Working Group in 1990 included a section on Equal Opportunities which recommended that:

'Teachers should have careful thought to differences in the historical roles of men and women and draw attention to them whenever appropriate...It is helpful to consider the implication of historical events to both men and women and to avoid the token lip service to the history of women. Our approach is intended to combat inherent stereotypes. Women should be studied not only as part of social history...but in contexts often treated as exclusively "male", such as politics, war, commerce and science. In this process the evidence for women's activities, often plentiful, should be heeded. In attempting to redress imbalances of perception through history teaching, it is important that the relation and interpretation of sources and topics should not become contrived or unbalanced in new ways.' (DES, 1990)

The Final Report offered examples of different women who could be studied, many of these unknown to most teachers. The model was somewhat contrived as these women had to fit into the framework of the PESC formula (Political, Economic, Social and Cultural history) and examples were given for each history study unit. This led to a wealth of sexist remarks in staff rooms and on courses about "dredging up unknown women just for the sake of it". If this model had survived, it could well have fallen into the trap of being contrived. However, once left out of the Final Order in April 1991, women such as St Hilda of Whitby, Frances Hodgson Burnett, Mary Jones and Mrs Gaskell failed to even be 'exemplary information' in the pressure of historical selection. Women once again became insignificant as National Curriculum history managed to edit them out through 'lack of time'.

Although reference was made in the final Order (DES, 1991) to equal opportunities issues it was much briefer than in the consultation documents and was left to the *Non-Statutory Guidance*. This pointed to the requirement to teach about the experiences of men and women and referred back to the History Working Group's statement that pupils should develop 'the quality of open-mindedness which questions assumptions and demands evidence for points of view'. It rather hopefully stated that:

'Classroom materials are now available which draw on (this) research and present an accurate view of women and minority groups in past societies.
The attainment targets require pupils to think about the limitations of evidence. Pupils might consider why evidence is sometimes

unavailable for the history of particular groups.' (NCC, 1991a)

Although reference to women's history was also clearly in the General Requirements of the Programmes of Study at Key Stages 2 and 3 it was not necessarily being delivered.

At the end of the first Year of National Curriculum History OFSTED were pointing out:

'At Key Stage 2, teachers frequently concentrated on the content of the Individual Study Units and largely ignored those aspects outlined in the General Requirements.' (OFSTED, 1993)

As Hilary Bourdillon in *'On The Record'* states:

'Simply to legislate that women's history is an important part of school history, will not change classroom practice unless teachers understand the subject and acquire the expertise to make it so.' (Bourdillon, 1994)

The official tone on issues became even more cautious with the Dearing Review in the *History Draft Proposals* (SCAA, 1994b) where gender issues were even more briefly stated. It was important to cut the National Curriculum so that it became manageable, but in doing so those cuts changed the emphasis and will possibly remove women still further from the pages of school history books. The only mentions of women in the *History Draft Proposals* were in the programme of study at Key Stage 1 where the lives of different kinds of *famous* men and women are mentioned, and in Key Stage 2 and Key Stage 3 where the requirement in the Key Elements was the same for both key stages, simply, 'that pupils should be taught about the experience of men and women in societies'. Some specific examples were given in the document. At Key Stage 2 in core study units 3 and 4 the introductory statement referred to men, women and children. In the Extension Unit D an in-depth study on, for example, Mary Queen of Scots or Mary Kingsley was suggested. The only specific example given at Key Stage 3 was in the study in depth in core study unit 4 on the 'Twentieth Century' where it was suggested that 'The Changing Role Of Women' might be used. All the other examples were of men. The inclusion of this example suggested that there could be some kind of progression in the study of women's history from that of individuals to that of the more general role of women. However, it was simply one of many examples and many schools would choose not to undertake such a study, especially if it overlapped with their current Social and Economic GCSE syllabus.

The revised *History Order* has continued with just the one mention of the lives of women at each Key Stage (DFE, 1995). At Key Stage 1 the requirement remains that 'Pupils should be taught about the lives of famous men and women'. At Key Stages 2 and 3 the Key Elements state that pupils should be taught about characteristics of particular periods and societies including the experiences of men and women and some progression in this is recognised. The Key Elements show progression from 'having a knowledge and understanding of the historical features' at Key Stage 2, to at Key Stage 3 being taught to 'analyse the features'. If progression through each part of all the Key Elements is included in schools' planning then in theory, there should be continuity in learning about the experiences of women.

Some obvious opportunities for studying the experiences of women at Key Stage 2 have been lost from the statutory requirements. With the cut from eight units down to six, extension unit D, the 'Study In Depth' unit, is lost and with it the opportunity to study the life of a woman in depth. Mary Queen of Scots and Mary Kingsley join the list of female casualties. At Key Stage 3 the opportunity to study the changing role and status of women in the twentieth century world remains as one example within a mass of other suggestions. There is just one addition in this whole gradually shrinking coverage of women's history in Unit 2 – in 'The Making of the United Kingdom', the changing role of women is added as an example of a social change.

The revised *History Order* is intended, however, only as 'a child's essential entitlement', as the School Curriculum and Assessment Authority (SCAA) are at pains to point out. The *History Order* is seen as simply a bare statuary minimum, now giving schools greater flexibility and choice, both within and without the statutory requirements. So it is still possible to teach about the history of women and about equal opportunities issues, but responsibility for that is with the schools to ensure that a broad and balanced curriculum is delivered. The cross-curricular elements now have a lower profile as they were not included in the Dearing Review and gender, as a cross-curricular dimension, is no longer an issue.

Carol Adams wrote in 1981 'Off The Record' about women's omission from classroom historical evidence:

'If the stuff on history with which pupils are engaged ranges from King Alfred to William the Conqueror, to Francis Drake to Hitler, then however developed the pupils ability to abstract the processes of historical study from the material may be, they are nonetheless dealing with the past of only one half of the human race and are therefore implicitly operating in a restricted historical field.' (Adams, 1981)

This has an all too familiar ring with the first few years experience of the implementation of National Curriculum History. Gilly Robson argued in 'Bebba and her Sisters':

> 'Women academics do not tackle the basic issue of the systematic misrepresentation of female achievement in a male dominated society.' (Robson, 1991)

It could be argued that despite laudable origins, neither does National Curriculum history.

Resources for teaching history

Textbooks for National Curriculum history have had a far greater impact on teaching than is acknowledged. The publication of the history National Curriculum in April 1991 led to a flood of new resources. Most schools recognised the importance of resourcing it and briefly primary and secondary teachers had larger budgets to spend on history resources than ever before. The funding was often time limited so teachers had to spend quickly.

At Key Stages 1 and 2 the lack of any resources previously produced meant that the new publications cornered the market. The impossibility of delivering history without sources, pictures and textbook ideas was soon recognised as primary teachers struggled to adapt unsuitable secondary material, whilst waiting for the publication of resources. At Key Stage 3, although many teachers already had sets of books on the Romans or Mediaeval Britain, the threat of Standard Assessment Task testing led many departments to buy the first available set of textbooks which seemed to cover the content and offer strategies for meeting the statements of attainment.

As never before, it is the Ginn, Longman, Heinemann and John Murray interpretations of National Curriculum History which pervade schools. It is often the awareness and approaches by the authors of the books on each history study unit which affects whether gender issues are included.

At Key Stage 1 resources and textbooks for the younger pupils, where they are looking at changes in their own lives and people around them, show little gender imbalance. In fact it is more often memories of women which are used in the classroom and often familiar objects from the home, which are still mainly used by women, which are brought in first as artefacts.

Oxford Primary History has introduced a 'Decades History Series' which concentrates on the lives of Katy's family in the past. The books are based around a real family and focus on the lives of the women and changes over time. It is when history leaps across that great divide into teaching pupils about 'the lives of different kinds of famous men and women'and 'helping pupils develop an awareness of the past through stories from different periods and cultures' that the gender inequalities become apparent. The real problem lies with the requirement to teach about the lives of famous people, as very few women are famous. Does this mean that women should remain invisible? The list of examples of rulers, saints, artists, engineers, explorers, inventors and pioneers could, without research into the less famous women, lead to the traditionally famous, white, middle-class chaps found in any 'Boys Own Handbook of History'.

It is hard to synthesise someone's whole life into a few pages that can be understood by the average six and a half year old. Often the result is not worth reading as it is so simplified that it becomes invalid. Oxford, Ginn and Heinemann have published biographies to try to help teachers address this difficult requirement. Both series have focused on some women, some men and some general experiences. The flag for women's history at Key Stage 1 rests with Emily Pankhurst, Princess Victoria, Orphan Mary, Boudicca and one token black woman, Mary Seacole. The other biographies try to include the experiences of women, some more successfully than others. Oxford's Primary History's *The Vikings* includes the views of two women compared with six men.

Key Stage 2 textbooks and Key Stage 2 teachers, to some extent, are not explicit in recognising women's history. The textbooks to a great extent seem to represent a reworking of the traditional issues in school history, only now with colour pictures. The texts often do not show an awareness of debate or of controversial issues.

HMI observed in *History in the Primary and Secondary Years*:

'History syllabuses have tended to focus on women in three ways: the struggle for women's rights in recent British history, the women who exceptionally became military and political leaders, such as Boadicea and Elizabeth 1, and women's work, usually manual work, in industry and households in the last two centuries. To restrict women's part in history to such topics is both to ignore and distort women's contributions to past societies.' (DES, 1985)

This remains the focus of many Key Stage 2 textbooks. Surprisingly, however, the number of pictures of men compared with women is less unbalanced than might be expected, although it is still giving clear visual messages to pupils about gender roles.

In general, in Key Stage 2 books on the Tudors and Stuarts the images of men outnumber women by over three to one (Table 6.1). Key Stage 2 authors have clearly been very careful to include as many pictures of women as possible, to the extent that 20% of the images in Oxford's *Tudor & Stuarts* are of women today. These are token illustrations showing women re-enacting 5th November or shopping in York. Most of the contemporary images show women as queens, ladies-in-waiting or as poor labourers. All the textbooks have significantly less images of women in Stuart times. Longman's *Tudor and Stuart Chronicle* is the only one to include a picture of Henrietta Maria and one of Lady Bankes, who defended Corfe Castle with her maid. Collins *Tudors and Stuarts* uses a picture with only one woman when showing 'The Pilgrim Fathers' and makes no reference to the fact that any of the 'Pilgrim Fathers' were

Textbook/publisher	Number of men shown	Number of women shown	Ratio of males to females
Tudors and Stuarts Collins	206	57	3.6:1
Tudor and Stuart Times Folens	188	33	5.6:1
Tudors and Stuarts Times Ginn	240	63	3.8:1
Tudor and Stuart Life Longman	178	86	2:1
Tudor and Stuart Chronicle Longman	231	35	6.6:1
Writing and Printing Oxford Primary History	243	57	4.2:1

Table 6.1 Numbers of visual images in some Key Stage 2 Tudor and Stuart textbooks

women. With such a poor gender ratio the colony would hardly have survived! In fact, of the 102 who sailed, 65 were men and the rest were women and children (Cowrie, 1970).

It is not surprising that a Year 4 class who had counted the number of male and female pictures in textbooks, when asked if there were more men than women in Stuart times, thought perhaps there were. One boy said that maybe only about 25% of the population were women. It is partly the political focus on the Stuart period which has lead to this picture of deficiency and partly that a traditional view of history is being presented. There is no lack of resources on women at this time. Islington Education Service have produced a very different view in their publication *Putting Women into the History Curriculum – Women in Tudor & Stuart Times* (Adler, 1993). The dropping of the Stuarts from this unit will have the effect of increasing the proportion of women studied but opportunities for junior school children to learn about women in Stuart times will have been lost.

Research shows that the proportion of male and female visuals in the 'Invaders and Settlers' unit is much the same as in the 'Tudors and Stuarts' but far worse are the textbooks on the now almost defunct 'Exploration and Encounters' unit. The role of women is almost entirely invisible. Only the role of Aztec townswomen has been recognised. Textbooks on 'Britain Since 1930' are slightly better on gender, with an average of about two men to one woman.

Given the power of visual images on pupils and the sheer number of resource packs which are being sold by the leading publishers, one of the oddest choices of posters must be the 'Home Front' image of women knitting and listening to the radio news in the Longmans *Sense of History* pack. The pack has just six posters to represent 'Britain since 1930s'. Having chosen to show women in the Second World War, why was this image chosen and the opportunity to show women in other roles lost? This question was asked at a GEST 11 funded course for primary teachers in Birmingham. First they were asked to brainstorm which image they would choose to represent the role of women the war. Their suggestions were:

• Women working in aircraft factories.
• "Join the ATS" poster.
• Land army photographs.
• A woman balancing ration books.

They were then asked what issues the poster from Longmans raised for them:

• The lady of the house isn't knitting.
• The blackout.
• The propaganda machine.

- Doing their bit.
- 'Make do and mend'.
- The power of the radio.
- Class differences.
- Solidarity with the men at the front.
- The drabness of the war.
- Women are passively waiting.
- Women are weak.
- Women keeping the home fires burning.
- Women work for poor soldiers.
- But above all: women depend on men!

Discussion around the choice of image to represent women in the war proved a successful INSET strategy and encouraged debate about the role of women in the war. This could also work in the classroom to give pupils the opportunity to discuss the impact of images, the power of selection and the lessons of omission. Although this surely was not the reason why it was chosen for the pack.

In her article 'Still Hidden From History? The Representation of Women in Recently Published History Text Books', Audrey Osler examined whether the new Key Stage 3 books were built upon equality initiatives and whether they are contributing to the development of history which is gender balanced. She concluded that the textbooks which she had reviewed:

'...have avoided some of the worst excesses of sexist language which were a feature of many books as recently as a decade ago. Although this represents progress, there is still a long way to go to achieve a more balanced historical record and to move closer towards a real understanding of the lives of women in the past. Textbook illustrations in particular indicate that the publishers need to give this issue further consideration.' (Osler, 1994)

Audrey Osler's study included an audit of illustrations in textbooks on 'The Roman Empire', 'The Medieval Realms' and 'The Making of the UK.', which showed that:

'...in every book the number of photographs of men far exceeded those of women, although there was considerable variation between the texts: the best balanced book (The Roman Empire, Spartacus) still had twice as many images of men as of women and in the least equitable examples, photographs of men outnumbered those of women by 26:1 or more.' (Osler, 1994)

The politically based units which deal with constitutional history are less likely to include a women's perspective than the social and economic units. Key Stage 3, despite the PESC formula has evolved with an over emphasis on politics. The unit on 'The Making of the UK', due to the focus of its content, on the changing relationship between crown and parliament, is one where women seem to be almost totally excluded. The life and influence of Queen Henrietta Maria is often dismissed in one pejorative sentence; soldiers and battles predominate rather than the effects of the Civil War on the people. Schools History Project 'Societies in Change' is one exception where the life of Lady Harley during the Civil War is a focus, but on one page only. The Women's Petition to the House of Commons in 1649 is ignored, as it was by Parliament who gave their answer that 'they desired the women to go home and look after their own business and meddle with their husbandry' (Miles, 1988).

If there is indeed a change in the role of women in the twentieth century then the visual images in the textbooks should be more balanced. However a review of visual images in the pre-Dearing unit 'The Era of the Second World War' textbooks (Table 6.2) still reveals a distinct gap between the numbers of images of men and those of women.

Textbook /publisher	Number of men shown	Number of women shown	Proportion of males to females
The Era of the Second World War Heinemann	196	39	**5:1**
The Era of the Second World War Hodder & Stoughton	311	113	**2.7:1**
Peace & War SHP (Section on WW2) John Murray	504	124	**5.2:1**
The Era of the Second World War Stanley Thornes	188	33	**5.2:1**

Table 6.2 Visual images. The Era of the Second World War

Perhaps it is the focus of the unit again on politics and on war. However, some books show women in an uncharacteristically passive role during the war. The SHP book, 'Peace and War' has only one double-page spread on women at war.

The debate in Key Stage 3 history textbooks is whether to integrate the experience of women into the study units or whether to have a 'couple of double page spreads on the role of women' and then to get on with 'history'.

Audrey Osler in her review of Key Stage 3 textbooks wrote:

'Although including a section on women is a small step towards achieving a more gender-balanced history, it could be argued that, without reviewing their policies on the representation of women as a whole, publishers run the risk of ghettoising issues relating to women.' (Osler, 1994)

She points out that Cambridge University Press had produced a special series 'Women in History' pre-national curriculum and that part of these could support teaching and learning, but women's issues have not been included in their main texts. The SHP have a separate book on *The Changing Role of Women* which had been produced as material for a category A Supplementary Unit. Much of the material in it could supplement the British History Units. Many teachers try to use women as examples whenever there is an opportunity rather than just one 'women's section'.

The BBC's *History File*, the series of programmes to support Key Stage 3 history, has made a deliberate attempt to redress ethnic and gender balances. A black woman is used as the 'time traveller' who introduces the programmes and at different stages through the series the words of women as well as men are given. Spoken sources are used. The words of the men are from one named source. The words of the women are also heard but these are essentially compilations of descriptions and words from a number of different people, so the characters of the ordinary women in the series are fakes.

Many historians might disagree with this distortion of reality and with this attempt at positive discrimination. At least, however, the attitudes of women are considered and women are not invisible.

Key Stage 3 textbook writers may argue that they are simply reflecting the past but in doing so are they continuing to offer an unbalanced curriculum which disempowers girls? The textbooks seem to have put an unintentional stranglehold on the development of women's history, but are schools and history teachers to some extent allowing this to happen?

There is little that teachers can do to alter the illustrations in the existing textbooks. They could write to publishers and hope that the next range of National Curriculum history books will take on the issues. However this seems unlikely as gender issues appear to be slipping from the national agenda. A far more important strategy is to alert pupils to the omission of women from text books, allow them to undertake their own research and to adopt a range of strategies to help pupils to challenge the stereotypes which will always exist, for themselves. The following strategies could be employed.

Figure 6.1 shows an example of research by some Year 7 lower ability pupils when examining textbooks on 'The Roman Empire'.

RESEARCHING TEXT BOOKS

Study the history text books and count the number of pictures which show

a) women and b) men

NUMBER OF WOMEN	NUMBER OF MEN 160

18
‖‖† ‖‖† ‖‖†
‖‖

Hate ‖‖† ‖‖† ‖‖† ‖‖‖
‖‖† ‖‖† ‖‖†
‖‖† ‖‖† ‖‖† ‖‖†
‖‖† ‖‖† ‖‖‖ ‖‖† ‖‖
‖‖† ‖‖† ‖‖† ‖‖†
‖‖† ‖‖† ‖‖‖ ‖‖† ‖‖†

WHAT ARE THE WOMEN IN THE PICTURES DOING?

The women are standing and some of them are pretty

WHAT ARE THE MEN IN THE PICTURES DOING?

In war   Talking   waiting
Gladiators   Riding horse   Spectators
Doc man
carrlyng animals

Figure 6.1 Year 7 lower ability pupils examining textbooks on the 'The Roman Empire

Why are women hardly noticed in history?

Some pupils at a Birmingham secondary school tried to think of the reasons why women are left out of history books:

'Our Suggestions:

- Most historians were men and they had sexist views. The earliest historians were monks.

- The jobs women did were taken for granted.

- Men always want the attention.

- Men were thought of as more important than women.

- Men didn't think that women were important enough to write about.

- Men thought women were second-class citizens and their place was in the home.

- Men thought they were doing more because they are physically stronger than women.

- Men held the most important and highest jobs like kings and bishops and they controlled the government.

- Men were dominant because they had all the official jobs and had all the weapons.

Year 8 mixed ability pupils'.

History 14–16

At Key Stage 4 the retention of the existing GCSE syllabuses for the time being means that some substantial studies on the changing role of women will remain. Ten years ago examination boards were pressurised into including options on women's history and the progress made in their inclusion could well have slipped from the agenda if the overcrowded and unrealistic proposals for Key Stage 4 history remained. The main opportunities in the most popular GCSE courses are in the 'Changing Role of Women' in the British Social & Economic history paper and as part of the History of Medicine in the School History Project syllabus. As a result women do tend to be pigeon-holed within these areas and it becomes almost a development study.

The unit on 'The changing role and status of women since 1700' in

MEG's Social and Economic history is now the third most popular topic on Paper 2. The history of women is only in this section in the Social and Economic history syllabus. Women should play a part throughout. Did Jenny Hargreaves help to invent the Spinning Jenny? How significant was the role of the Matchgirls in the history of Trade Unions? Why did advances in midwifery have to wait for William Smellie to validate them? The question again is whether to integrate or to separate. The answer of course should be to do both.

Studying the 'Changing Role of Women' and indeed the 'Evolution of the Multi-cultural Society in Britain' is slightly different from studying the other topics at GCSE as a shift in attitude from the pupils is expected at the end of the course, as well as the acquisition of knowledge. Although it is not desirable that pupils should harbour racist views, having studied the topic on the 'Evolution of the Multi-cultural Society in Britain', it can hardly be penalised. In the topic on the 'Changing Role of Women' pupils often respond to the injustice of the source rather than responding to its usefulness or its reliability as evidence. Attitudes cannot be credited in examinations, only a weighing up of historical evidence. This often misleads weaker candidates. A clear example was in a source used in the 1991 examination where candidates were asked about the usefulness of this source to anyone studying the place of women in the nineteenth century:

Source C.
"An old folk song about a ploughman's wife."

There was a little man came from the West,
He married a wife, she was not the best.

She wouldn't card, she wouldn't spin,
She wouldn't work all in the kitchen.

When this good man came home from plough,
He say, "My dear, is dinner ready now?"

"Oh if your dinner you must have,
Then get it yourself, I am not your slave.

For I won't brew and I won't bake
And I won't get my white hands black."

This good man pulled his coat from his back,
And made his stick go widgy, widgy wack.

"And if you won't do what I say now
I'll take and yoke you to the plough."

"Oh I will card and I will spin,
And I will work in the kitchen.

And I will bake and I will brew,
And I will cook the dinner for you!"

(MEG, 1991)

Many weaker candidates wrote about how much they disagreed with the source, rather than seeing it as an historical document about the treatment of women which was common at the time. The examination paper is asking students to ignore their own attitudes and simply to concentrate on the source but the teacher is hoping that pupils will be able to develop both.

If all pupils were to study an option on the role of women at Key Stage 4 then there would be a progressive experience from 5 to 16. However, many pupils give up history at 14. Hence perhaps the decision to include the 'changing role of women' as a suggested study in depth at Key Stage 3. Even if pupils continue with history they may not study an option on women. The Modern World syllabus for example does not provide the same opportunities for looking at women's roles.

The draft proposals for GCSE Criteria for History suggest that each syllabus should enable the study of:

'Where appropriate, the social, cultural, religious and ethnic diversity of the societies studied and the experiences of men and women in those societies.' (SCAA, 1994m)

The corollary 'where appropriate' suggests the optional nature of any study of ethnic diversity or of the experiences of women. So a progressive experience is possible but far from statutory.

History Policies and Equal Opportunities Issues

With OFSTED and the 'threat' of inspection, history policies are being produced and updated in many primary and secondary schools. The *Non-Statutory Guidance* for history, included equal opportunities in its guidance in what to include in a history curriculum plan (NCC, 1991a). At present it is OFSTED and the inspection process which are ensuring that equal opportunities statements are included in school curriculum policies. Equal opportunities are firmly on the agenda in the *Handbook for the Inspection of Schools* (OFSTED, 1993b). It is stressed in section 7.3(ii) on Equality of Opportunity and in 5.1 on 'Pupils' spiritual, moral, social and cultural development' and through references to cross-curricular elements. Many schools have written or are rewriting policies which on paper show that they are addressing equal opportunities through their history curriculum. Included in these policies is often the importance of looking at women in history and a bland statement about 'equal opportunities for all, regardless of race, gender or special needs.' Many go no further and the policy has little effect on practice.

It is the implementation of equal opportunities policies which is far more difficult. This is possibly because it works on different levels. It is about the content; about including women in the syllabuses and being aware of inequalities or misconceptions. It is also about how far teachers have developed their own awareness, how far they can tackle the issues and have reviewed their own language and attitudes. Equally important are teaching methods, classroom interaction, girls' achievement and a whole-school approach to gender issues.

An effective policy, ideally, should show how teachers plan work, how they organise and manage classes to take account of the different needs of pupils and how they maintain consistently high expectations. The guidance on History has no specific reference but in referencing the 'Quality of Learning' the appropriate attitudes and values which pupils should demonstrate are those which would foster equal opportunities:

'appropriate attitudes and values: a sense of the past and an awareness of how the past has helped to fashion the present: an enthusiasm for exploring the past; respect for evidence; toleration of a range of opinions; a constructive approach to collaborative working.' (OFSTED, 1993b)

Genderwatch, After the Education Reform Act (Myres, 1992) offers many useful suggestions to teachers and helps teachers to review their practice and move forward. Some secondary Birmingham teachers on a Curriculum Support Service course on 'Herstory' produced these principles to ensure equal opportunities in the history curriculum:

'It is important to recognise that:

● Women should not necessarily be judged against the same criteria of "achievement" as men. There should be a debate about "achievement".
● It's not enough to pick out a few token women (although it is better

than making no mention of them).

- If women's history is left out the contribution of women will remain invisible.
- Women are still working towards equal opportunities.
- How girls and women are treated in school is also significant.
- Sexist behaviour needs to be recognised as an important issue and tackled.
- Gender issues need to be tackled in history as part of a whole-school approach to equal opportunities.'

Examples of equal opportunities statements from two Birmingham secondary history departments are included. The first illustrates a willingness to review and rethink and the second, the different aspects which equal opportunities needs to be addressing.

'Equal Opportunities

This department continues to be committed to equalising opportunity.

We believe that the experience of men and women, of different cultures and socio-economic backgrounds should be at the heart of history and that these considerations should be essential in the planning, delivery and evaluation of lessons and schemes of work. This department was firmly behind the move to put women back into history. The department developed schemes of work which provided opportunity for the role of women to be discussed in a classroom context. Indeed, an entire scheme of work looking at Women Through History was planned and implemented prior to the onset of National Curriculum.

The department now feels that the time has come to review its current policy, and to evaluate its success and to amend if appropriate.

While recognising that putting women back into history was a crucial step, we now feel that in some ways this process has been self-defeating. There is a danger of compartmentalising women.'

Another department, having examined the content of their history syllabus for gender bias, has taken on these other aspects:

'This Department will endeavour to:

2.2   Pupil Experiences

2.2.1   Give all pupils, irrespective of ability, gender, race, special needs, social and cultural background, equal opportunities in all aspects of Humanities.

2.2.2 Give consideration to the make up of class sets so that wherever possible and desirable, a balance between gender groups can be achieved and ensure that all options on offer by the Department are open to all pupils.

2.3 Departmental Monitoring

2.3.1 Check textbooks regularly for sexual or racial bias, and improve whenever possible; and to cater for those with special educational needs and differing abilities.

2.3.2 Monitor the language used by staff and pupils, so that racial/sexual stereotyping can be countered.

2.4 Teacher Experiences

2.4.1 Promote equality of opportunity in the appointment and promotion of staff, and the allocation of tasks within the Department.

2.4.2 Adopt classroom management styles and teaching methodologies which positively encourage all students.

2.5 Evaluation

2.5.1 Evaluate this policy on a regular basis.

History Department.'

In the *Handbook for the Inspection of Schools* inspectors are advised that in judging how effectively policies are implemented:

'The core task is to assess the influence of the school's practice and policies on pupils' access to the curriculum and their achievements.' (OFSTED, 1993b)

In terms of implementing equal opportunities through the history curriculum pupils would ideally be demonstrating that gender issues were being addressed through:

• having acquired knowledge about women in history;
• being able to challenge stereotypes in textbooks, sources etc.;
• showing a toleration of different opinions;
• having the confidence to ask questions and to challenge assumptions;
• being able to work constructively and co-operatively in different groups, mixed gender or single sex;

- girls demonstrating appropriate achievement and making effective curriculum choices.

Planning for continuity in the teaching of gender issues

In *Teaching History at Key Stage 3* NCC set out an INSET activity designed to consider ways of planning work to ensure progression and continuity in pupils' understanding of historical situations. Part of that task was to look at identified topics from a unit then to see how far they met the General Requirements (NCC, 1993c). This idea could be taken a step further so that learning about the experiences of women is planned, not just through a single study unit, but across a whole Key Stage. *Teaching History at Key Stage 2* (NCC, 1993b) sets out a framework for achieving coherence across the whole key stage, related to the general requirements. This framework provides the opportunity to see where social, cultural and ethnic diversity and the experiences of men and women might be covered through each study unit. This again could be taken another step further so that it maps delivery across all key stages. For most schools an analysis of the coverage of women in history would be a salutary experience. Ideally it should provide a continuous and coherent thread leading towards a more progressive, planned learning experience. To do this, however, cross-phase links would have to be made.

Tables 6.3–6.6 suggest how gender issues might be tackled through the years, building on from early experiences, involving listening to memories, then learning about individual women and developing to learning about women within societies. At secondary schools pupils would then look at women's' achievements in a wider context and at inequalities and the process of selection in history. In Year 9 and at GCSE this would develop into a wider and critical study of the role of women and how far women's roles have changed.

Using this kind of framework across the key stages would help to monitor implementation and also develop attitudes and break down stereotypes consistently from the early years. Teachers would automatically be looking for examples which include women. By the time pupils reach the age of 5 many prejudices are already firmly in place. Questioning the role of women in society cannot wait for a GCSE course. This kind of review, ideally, should also include a monitoring of classroom activities, monitoring the responses of girls compared with boys, reviewing images in textbooks and using wall displays to break down stereotypes and presenting positive images of girls' achievements.

Table 6.3 Key Stage 1

Reception	Ourselves	Personal timelines, birthdays. Stories about the passing of time. (Examples of girls and ethnic minorities.) Artefacts – Things I don't use any more, e.g. baby clothes, broken toys.
	Toys	Special toys without gender bias.
	Homes	Homes – different homes. Work in the home.
Year 1	Our families	Women and men in families. Listening to memories.
	People who help us	Questioning role assumptions.
Year 2	Famous people	Working women in the past. Important women, Mary Seacole etc.
	The local area – how we used to live	Girls and boys in Victorian times.

Table 6.4 Key Stage 2

Year 3	The Egyptians	Women in Egyptian Society, Cleopatra
	The Greeks	Greek women. Democracy?
Year 4	Invaders (Roman Focus)	Boudicca. Women and settlement
	Local Study	Women in the local area
Year 5	Tudors	Queens and ordinary people – Using evidence
	Exploration and Encounters	Filipa Columbus, Queen Isabella, Aztec Women
Year 6	Victorians	Queen Victoria – roles of women, rich and poor. Women in the factories and coal mines
	Britain since 1930	Women in the Second World War. Changing lives of women since the war

Table 6.5 Key Stage 3

Year 7	Roman Empire	Reviewing textbooks. The roles of Roman women
	Medieval Realms	Working women. Life in convents
Year 8	Making of the UK	Elizabeth I. Henrietta Maria. Why are women 'left out' in the Civil War?
	Black Women and Men of the Americas	Women in the Americas. Prejudice and inequality
Year 9	Britain 1750–1900	Women in the Industrial Revolution. The Match Girls
	The Twentieth Century world	Women in the wars, including black women in wars. Why did women return to traditional roles after the war? The changing role and status of women.

Table 6.6 Key Stage 4. British Social and Economic Syllabus (MEG)

Year 10	Industrial Development and Course Work	Women's roles in the Domestic System. Women in industry. Effect of Factory Acts on Women
Year 11	Topic E	Has equality now been achieved?
	The Changing roles and Status Women Since 1700	Has equality now been achieved?

The way forward

To some extent it is the fault of the National Curriculum that gender issues are slipping from the agenda. Some teachers admit that gender issues have dropped as a priority since its introduction as they now see it as just one of number of criteria which they are trying to address. To some extent, however, the fault lies with teachers for being too conscientious in their interpretation of the Order.

The revised Order now leaves a much slimmer, more flexible curriculum and one which gives teachers far more initiative. The experiences of women still remain within National Curriculum history, with some progression through the Key Elements. Equal opportunities are still an integral part of the inspection process. More resources for teaching about the experiences of women are gradually becoming available for all key stages, although there is a long way to go before there is a balanced, coherent coverage. Above all, history which includes everyone is good history. Just because National Curriculum history no longer gives women's history and gender issues a high priority, does not mean that teachers cannot, and indeed will not, teach it.

Acknowledgements

Thanks to teachers and pupils from: Golden Hillock Secondary School, Bishop Walsh RC Secondary School and Dorrington Junior and Infant School.

Teachers from: Archbishop Ilsley RC School (Glen Alexander), Regents Park J & I School (Sue Collins), Shenley Court Secondary School (Tony Morrison) and Swanshurst Girls Secondary School (Prue Morrison).

Participants on Birmingham History GEST 11 for Key Stage 2 teachers, run by Birmingham University and Birmingham Curriculum Support Service. Participants on Curriculum Support Service History Courses.

Useful Resources

Adams, C., *et al.* (eds) (1989) *Women In History* Series. Cambridge: Cambridge University Press.

Adler, S. *et al.* (eds) (1993) *Putting Women Into The History Curriculum. Women In Tudor and Stuart Times*. Islington Education Service and Islington Women's Equality Unit.

Bellamy, L. and Morse, K. (1994) *The Changing Role of Women*. Schools

History Project.

BBC Education (1993) *History File*

Fawcett, V., *et al.* (1993) *Family History Books*. Oxford: Oxford University Press.

Haritos, A. (ed.) (1992) *1492 The Role Of Women. Women in Europe Supplements* Vol. 37. Commission of the European Communities

Myres, K. (ed.) (1992) *Genderwatch after the Education Reform Act.* Oxford : Oxford University Press.

Reynoldson, F. (1994) *Victorian Women Abroad*. Harlow: Longman

7

Ensuring continuity and understanding through the teaching of enquiry and communication in history, 5–16

Chris Palmer

History is the communication now of some or other aspects of the past. It is more than simply the past expressing itself through what it has left behind. What has been left behind – artefacts, documents, buildings and sites, or any other of the sources specified for National Curriculum history – does not really contribute to history until it is placed in a context and explained by the historian. When the historian does this, these relics of the past become evidence. But this process is not unproblematic. As Brian Garvey and Mary Krug put it:

> '...the relics of history are not like a jig-saw puzzle in which every piece eventually finds its place. They are more like the contents of a box of odd pieces, and it is often difficult to see whether all the pieces belong to one puzzle or to several. The historian's art is to produce meaning from a jumble of evidence, to create order out of what sometimes resembles chaos. And to teach pupils...to create such order is to train them in a basic historical skill.' (Garvey and Krug, 1977)

This is similar in many respects to what E. H. Carr wrote when trying to answer the question 'What is history?':

> 'The nineteenth century fetishism of facts was completed and justified by a fetishism of documents. The documents were the Ark of the Covenant in the temple of facts. The reverent historian approached them with bowed head and spoke of them in awed tones. If you find it in the documents it is so. But what, when we get down to it, do these

documents…tell us?…None of this means anything until the historian has got to work on it and deciphered it. The facts, whether found in documents or not, have still to be processed by the historian before he can make any use of them: the use he makes of them is, if I may put it that way, the processing process.' (Carr, 1964)

Carr went on to add that, 'facts and documents are essential to the historian. But…they do not by themselves constitute history' (Carr, 1964).

In this way, the twin processes of enquiry into these sources and communication of one's findings are at the heart of historical learning, the development of historical knowledge, skills and understanding. They are the interaction between the historian and the evidence, the dialogue between the present and the past. They are crucial to effective historical education in schools.

Enquiry is the process through which young historians will come to terms with issues like cause and consequence, change and continuity, features of historical periods and the different ways in which history can be and has been interpreted. It is central to a developing ability to use historical sources, which are the raw materials for reaching such understanding. This learning and developing understanding of history then has to be communicated to others. Communication, in this way, is the other central element at the heart of the development of historical understanding. It is also central to assessment. Communication, however, is not merely the same as children writing down what they know about the past. There is sometimes a tendency to associate history with the written word, with books, but this is only one approach. This is something which will be further explored in the course of this chapter.

Despite the importance of these two issues in the study of history, they have enjoyed a somewhat chequered history in terms of National Curriculum history. From a proposed fourth attainment target for history, they were relegated to a short statement in the general requirements for each key stage. With the Dearing Review, however, they underwent something of a renaissance. They are now central features of the Key Elements at each key stage, which provide the basis for planning, teaching and learning, the devising of activities and day-to-day assessment in the new curriculum. They are recognisable aspects of the level descriptions for the new history attainment target, even though not all aspects of progression in enquiry and communication are featured in these descriptions. It is also the case that the former attainment target 3, concerning sources, in the previous Order has now been effectively integrated into Key Elements 4 and 5, 'Historical enquiry' and 'Organisation and communication' respectively. This is generally a more satisfactory arrangement.

At Key Stage 1, children need to see historical study as a process of finding out about the past from the range of specified sources they have at their disposal. To do this they need to develop the skills of questioning: asking questions like:

● Why did that happen?
● Why did she or he do that?
● What was that used for?
● How did they do that?
● What is the difference between that object and one we use to do the same thing today?

These questions will not always come naturally to children. At least in the early years, teachers will need to lead and develop this questioning process. As the new Order states, pupils should be taught:

'a. how to find out about aspects of the past from a range of sources of information, including artefacts, pictures and photographs, adults talking about their own past, written sources, and buildings and sites;

b. to ask and answer questions about the past.' (DFE, 1995)

An example of this might be children looking at a picture of an old horse drawn bus and comparing that bus with those with which they are familiar today, identifying, for example, the use of horses rather than an engine, the absence of a roof, the staircase being outside rather than inside. Figures 7.1 and 7.2 show examples of how an enquiry of this kind might be communicated. Figure 7.1 is from a reception class, while Figure 7.2 is from Year 1. In the reception example, there is no writing yet certain key features of a past situation have still been recognisably communicated: the absence of a roof and so on. In the Year 2 example, the child has used labels to identify more clearly the same features. Both pieces of work are based on systematic questioning with the pupils concerned, based on the central question, 'What is different?' As has already been suggested, at this stage, this questioning has to be led by the teacher, with the expectation that pupils will later learn to apply the same questioning process themselves.

If enquiry skills are to be developed successfully, these sources of information need to be kept as tangible and concrete as possible. Artefacts are crucial. Children can look at a picture of an old iron, they can look at a photograph of someone using one, but it is only when they have a real one to pick up and hold, feel how heavy it is, that it really comes to life and prompts more wide-reaching enquiry and, inevitably, more to

Figure 7.1

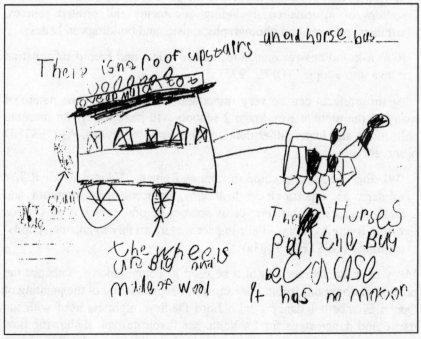

Figure 7.2

communicate. This is an issue which OFSTED have considered important and on which they have noted improvements:

> 'Many of the schools had made the acquisition and use of artefacts in the teaching and learning of history a priority and had built up extensive collections...In addition, teachers were also beginning to extend the scope of resources by, for example, using reproductions of portraits or historical paintings of historical events. Almost inevitably such material increased the pupils' interest in history and enhanced the quality of their learning. A minority of the schools, however, still ignored the potential benefits of using artefacts in their teaching.' (OFSTED, 1993a)

As pupils progress through Key Stage 2, these questions need to be sharpened and made more precise. They need support to develop research and study skills that help them to both find and record information, and then to sort, organise and analyse it. This information might come from school resource centres and libraries, or a variety of sources including visits to historical sites or visitors to schools. Perhaps the increasing number of multimedia computers which allow access to a wealth of historical sources and information on CD ROM can help in this situation. As the new Order states, pupils should be taught :

> 'a. how to find out about aspects of the periods studied, from a range of sources of information, including documents and printed sources, artefacts, pictures and photographs, music, and buildings and sites;
>
> b. to ask and answer questions, and to select and record information relevant to a topic.' (DFE, 1995)

Again artefacts can be very important, although given the nature of many of the units at Key Stage 2 schools will have to rely on museum collections and loans rather than on their own collections. As OFSTED observed:

> 'Whether the visitors came in role, as Romans, Vikings or Civil War soldiers; as experts: local historians, archaeologists, museum and archive education officers; or as sources of oral evidence on periods within living memory – their impact was invariably to enhance pupils' learning.' (OFSTED, 1993a)

Many of these sources can also be used in combination to enhance the process of communication. For example, a reproduction of the painting of Queen Elizabeth I dancing with Lord Dudley might be used with the music and dance steps for La Volta, her favourite dance, showing how sources can complement each other and help build a more detailed picture of an aspect of a particular period.

The process of questioning itself also needs attention and children need to be helped to consider what sorts of questions will elicit useful information. The teacher here needs to be a role model for effective questioning and often to be the leader of such questioning.

At Key Stage 3, this process needs to become more independent, and students need to develop the ability to refine questions for themselves in the light of their investigations.

As the new Order states pupils should learn:

'a. to investigate independently aspects of the periods studied, using a range of sources of information, including documents and printed sources, artefacts, pictures, photographs and films, music and oral accounts, buildings and sites;

b. to ask and answer questions, to evaluate sources in their historical context, identify sources for an investigation, collect and record information relevant to a topic and reach conclusions.' (DFE, 1995)

An important feature here is the word 'independently', which marks the importance, at Key Stages 3 and 4, of children increasingly becoming independent learners. However, as OFSTED noted, the range of sources used at Key Stage 3 can be somewhat limited, and this can diminish the scope of enquiry possible:

'Few departments had collections of historical artefacts. Of the minority which did, only a handful had broad collections.... Where such collections existed, they had considerable potential to enhance historical learning.... The use of out of school resources was also unsatisfactory in the majority of schools. In a large number of cases, Key Stage 3 pupils visited no historic sites or museums, or had only one such opportunity. On the other hand a minority of the departments showed considerable commitment and enterprise in this area of their work.... The pupils undoubtedly benefited from these learning opportunities, not least in the interest generated and the information recalled after the visit.' (OFSTED, 1993a)

If this is true at Key Stage 3, it is even more true of 'Key Stage 4'.

There is not, however, an inevitable dichotomy between children engaging themselves in a process of enquiry and the teacher imparting knowledge, information and interpretations of the past to children. Indeed, as the guidance for the inspection schedule for history notes, 'Good teaching in history provides a balance between imparting information to pupils through, for example, story and narrative, and prompting them to become active enquirers on their own account' (OFSTED, 1993b).

Similarly, as HMI have pointed out, 'There is an important and central place in history for 'good stories, well told' for narrative offered by teachers, and by pupils – and for pupils being taught to listen carefully and critically' (DES, 1988).

The development of pupils' skills in using sources is, however, just as important. In the limited time available within the National Curriculum for the study of history, children using a process of enquiry will only get very partial and potentially distorted views of the past. We must avoid a situation which may be compared with studying in detail a piece of bark on a tree trunk without knowing what the whole tree looks like, let alone the fact that it is in a forest. There are times when we as teachers will need to give an overview that allows the process of enquiry to take place in a meaningful way. We are, after all, teachers and not simply the suppliers of resources.

The new level descriptions, as has been mentioned already, do not exemplify every aspect of the Key Elements, but do contain the following partial progression:

- Level 1 – They are beginning to find answers to questions about the past from sources of information.
- Level 2 – They answer questions about the past, from sources of information, on the basis of simple observations.
- Level 3 – They find answers to questions about the past by using sources of information in ways that go beyond simple observations.
- Level 4 – They are beginning to select and combine sources of information.
- Level 5 – Pupils are beginning to evaluate sources of information and identify those that are useful for particular tasks.
- Level 6 – They identify and evaluate sources of information, which they use critically to reach and support conclusions.
- Level 7 – Pupils are beginning to show independence in following lines of enquiry, using their knowledge and understanding to identify, evaluate and use sources of information critically. They are beginning to reach substantiated conclusions independently.
- Level 8 – They use sources of information critically, carry out enquiries about historical topics, and independently reach substantiated conclusions. (DFE, 1995)

The central features of progression here are moves from answering questions based on observation (levels 1 and 2), to beginning to make deductions (level 3), to selecting and combining information (level 4), to the evaluation and increasingly critical assessment of sources (levels 5 and 6) through to an increasingly independent approach and the ability to substantiate their own conclusions (levels 7 and 8). What must be borne in mind is the relative difficulty of different sources, which was always a problem when assessing work against the old attainment target 3. A complex written source is clearly not appropriate for work at levels 1 and 2, while two Victorian irons would probably be inadequate, certainly by themselves, for addressing level 6.

The draft GCSE criteria fit into this kind of progression. For instance, to achieve Grade F pupils are required to, 'comprehend sources and, taking them at their face value, begin to consider their usefulness for investigating historical issues and draw simple conclusions'. To achieve Grade C this becomes, 'with reference to their historical context, evaluate and use sources to investigate issues and draw relevant conclusions', while to achieve Grade A it becomes, 'evaluate and use critically a range of sources in their historical context, to investigate issues and reach reasoned and substantiated conclusions' (SCAA, 1994m).

The evolving process of communication will mirror these developments in terms of enquiry. The new Order places much more emphasis than the old on the issue of language, starting from the common requirement of all the National Curriculum programmes of study relating to the use of language:

'Pupils should be taught to express themselves clearly in both speech and writing and to develop their reading skills. They should be taught to use grammatically correct sentences and to spell and punctuate accurately in order to communicate effectively in written English.' (DFE, 1995)

It is important, of course, that this statement should not be taken to mean that the only valid historical activities are those which focus on speech and writing.

At Key Stage 1, a major means of communication will be talk and probably drawing. The new Order states, pupils should be taught, 'to communicate their awareness and understanding of history in a variety of ways' (DFE, 1995). This marks a revision on the proposals, which included specific reference to oral and visual as well as written communication but it is still fair to assume that many pupils will be better able to demonstrate their growing historical knowledge and understanding through means of communication other than in writing. The child who produced the work in Figure 7.1, for example, could not

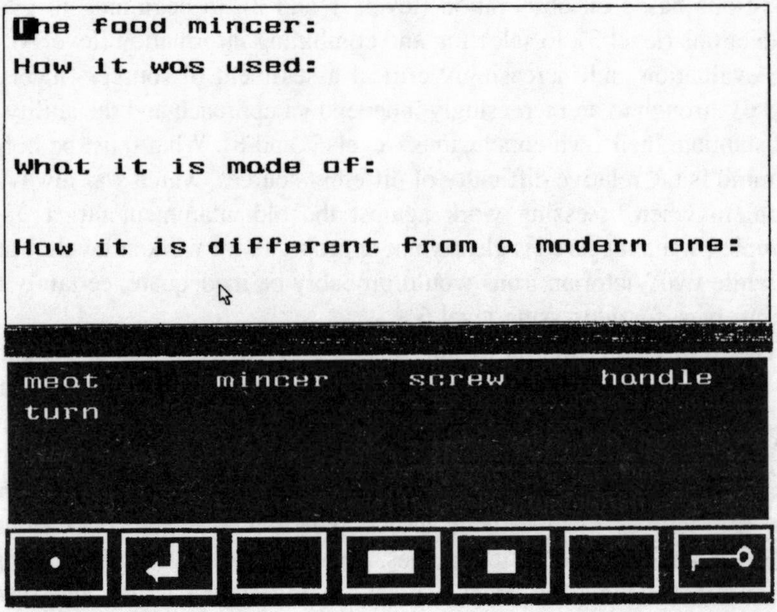

122

```
The food mincer:
How it was used:


What it is made of:

How it is different from a modern one:
                    ⤷
```
```
  meat        mincer      screw      handle
  turn
```
[·] [↵] [ ] [▭] [■] [ ] [⌐○]

Figure 7.3

have communicated similar knowledge and understanding in writing.

Children can talk about their own memories of toys they used to play with or what it used to be like at playgroup. They can do a labelled drawing like those in Figures 7.1 and 7.2. They can word process, perhaps using a concept keyboard or a word processor that allows children to select from word lists, as in Figure 7.3. Beside being effective history work in its own right, this kind of approach also addresses the common requirement to all National Curriculum programmes of study relating to all pupils being given opportunities to develop information technology capability.

In the case of Figure 7.3, the work was developed around the use of an old Victorian food mincer, one of the easiest of artefacts to acquire. Using a mouse, the child is able to insert relevant words from the word banks at the bottom of the screen to produce sentences about the irons. Also, the Key Stage 1 history Standard Assessment Tasks provide several useful approaches to communication. These are not only useful at Key Stage 1, but can be adapted for use across the Key Stages.

As children progress through Key Stage 2, the ability to communicate developing historical understanding through the written word will obviously become increasingly important, including, as the new Order requires, 'structured narratives and descriptions' (DFE, 1995). This should not be seen, however, as the pinnacle of achievement in terms of communication. Debates and drama can be just as important. As the National Curriculum Council wrote:

'Variety is not only important to maintain interest and motivation, but also because without a combination of activities, pupils will not be able to show breadth of understanding.... The choice of activity should be guided by the nature of the ideas the teacher is trying to teach.' (NCC, 1993c)

If children are to be encouraged to develop the ability to communicate in writing then they need to be helped: a blank piece of paper can be terribly daunting. The Key Stage 1 history Standard Assessment Tasks can be usefully adapted and provide children with structures which enable them to communicate effectively. Figures 7.4–7.6 show examples of work at Key Stage 2 which offer such structures. They are based on the story *Richard Grenville's Treasure*, which is first re-told (Figure 7.4). Richard's motivation is then considered (Figure 7.5) and finally previous knowledge is used to consider the idea of change and continuity, using Richard Grenville's house, a Roman house which had been studied in the previous academic year, and a modern house (Figure 7.6).

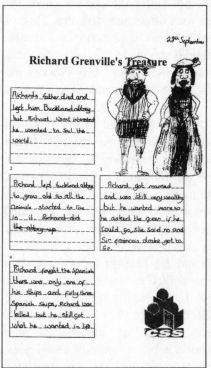

Figure 7.4

Figure 7.5

Changes

	A house in Roman times	A house in Tudor times	A house today
lighting	Oil lamps	~~Candl~~ Candals	Electric light
heating	Camp fire	Open fire	Gas fire
walls	Stone	Wood filled with Wattle & Daub.	bricks/Concrete
roof	straw.	Thatch	Tiles
cooking	Open fire	Spit fire.	Electric/Gas.
floors	Tiles.	Ground patted down.	Floor boards.

Can you think of some reasons for these changes?

Figure 7.6

The significant issue here is that the process of communication has been structured for children. They do not suffer the oppression of the blank sheet of paper, but are provided with limits and structure. This, of course, is not unique to Key Stage 2 as Figure 7.7, an example of similar work with less able pupils at Key Stage 3, shows. In this case, the work was part of a study of different versions of the story of Guy Fawkes and is based on a similar activity used in the Key Stage 1 Standard Assessment Tasks for History.

Pupils will also need increasingly to be introduced to the historical vocabulary that will facilitate this communication. As the new Order states, pupils should be taught, 'the terms necessary to describe the periods and topic studied, including court, monarch, parliament, nation, civilisation, invasion, conquest, settlement, conversion, slavery, trade, industry, law' (DFE, 1995). This is not necessarily difficult, provided pupils can cope with the concepts involved. They usually have no great difficulty in learning the terms used to describe them.

Of course, eventually children should be enabled as part of their curriculum entitlement to develop the ability to write more extensive pieces of continuous prose and this is something which has to be addressed at Key Stage 3, where a wider range of types of communication is needed. The new Order requires pupils, 'to communicate their knowledge and understanding of history, using a range of techniques, including extended narratives and descriptions, and substantiated explanations' (DFE, 1995).

Telling the story

Draw three pictures that tell the story of Guy Fawkes. Draw one picture from the beginning of the story, one from the middle and then one from the end. Then draw another picture of something else you could have drawn from the middle of the story. Add a caption to each picture. Then compare your pictures with those someone else has drawn. Mark each picture S if they are the same, D if they are different and SD if they are partly the same and partly different.

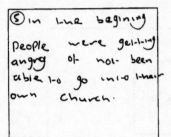

(S) In the begining people were getting angry ot not been able to go into their own church.

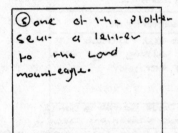

(S) one of the plotter sent a letter to the Lord mount-eagle.

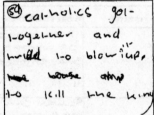

(SD) catholics got-together and wield to blow up, the house and to kill the king.

(S) guy fawkes got caught just before he lit the gun powder. he got tortured and quartered

Figure 7.7

This implies something more than reading a page of the textbook and answering a few questions, particularly if pupils are to be properly prepared for the requirements of GCSE examinations at Key Stage 4 when, 'Each scheme of assessment should provide opportunities for candidates to demonstrate achievement in a variety of ways and require candidates to write in extended prose' (SCAA, 1994m). Indeed, with course work restricted to 25%, the demands of writing become even more important. Thus, just as at Key Stage 2, offering a structure is critical. The following examples show a process in action during an investigation of aspects of the home front during World War II as part of a Key Stage 3 study. Students were first asked (Figure 7.8) how they thought types of sources might provide them with information to help them decide whether or not they accepted a particular view. Then (Figure 7.9) they looked at

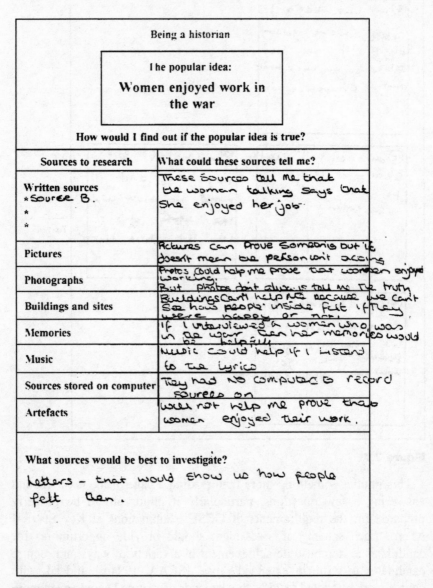

Figure 7.8

Do the sources support the idea?

Sources	Yes	No	Maybe	Because
Written				
*				
*				
*				
Pictures		A	✓	Because the person painting are the picture could have painted it with the person happy
Photographs			✓	Some photos show us the truth but some photos could be a act.
Buildings and sites		✓		Because they don't show us how people inside felt.
Memories	✓			memories can help me if I interviewd a Person (women) Who was in the war
Music				
Sources stored on computer		✓		Because they had No Computer to store information on.
Artefacts		✓		No Because it won't tell me how people felt.

Figure 7.9

sources before (Figure 7.10) moving on to a longer piece of writing communicating their findings. This systematic work, utilising in later communication the findings of earlier source-based work, proved effective not just in producing longer pieces of writing but in ensuring this writing made explicit use of relevant sources.

128

What do these sources tell you about women and work in World War II? What problems did
what they had to do cause women? Make reference to the sources to support your answer.

These sources show us that women have changed
a lot during the second world war.
~~Can a warden be a good wife?~~ This source is
advertising Mrs peeks foddings This appealed to the
people (women) who worked as a warden who couldn't
Provide their husbands with a hot dinner.
Women became more independant.
The poster which says "women of Britian come into
the factories" is asking "people (women) to work in
the factories to help their country to make ammunition
for England she is practically begging people to come
and work in the factories.
This sources: a) From designing gowns to making guns -
   b) your country needs you
   c) Medals for house wifes
   c) Can a warden be a good wife.
   d) Woman Farmers can't grow all your
       vegtables Dig for victory!!!
   e) Be a real commando of industry a
       night shift worker
   f) your eyes are doing double time.
   g) women of Britian come into factories.
Mainly appeal to women who were at home
during the war. They had to do the work
which the men left behind when they went
to fight the war for England.
Women had a hard time some/had to work
day and night diffrent shifts. ✓
They really did have a hard time but after
the war when the men came back they expected
the women to give everything up and go back to normal.
The women had to much independance to just drop every thing
but thats another story.
I did not get all my sources information from the booklet
I did some extra research to find out more. ✓?

Figure 7.10

In more general terms, extended written responses might be constructed thus:

1. What are the key features of …?
2. How do we know?
3. How did these features change?
4. Why did they change?
5. Does everybody agree on this or are there other versions?

Another important technique that unites the processes of enquiry and communication, at all Key Stages, is the use of DARTs activities. DARTs activities were developed by the DARTS project. The acronym means Directed Activities Related to Texts. For further information about DARTs see the various School's Council Project publications on the effective use of reading published by Heinemann between 1973 and 1976. Such activities focus children on texts and other materials to help develop an understanding beyond literal comprehension.

The following is an example based on a study of India, as part of a study of a non-European society at Key Stage 3:

'The Swadeshi Movement.

Cheap goods were made by machines in factories in Britain. They were sent to India and sold at a profit. The British wouldn't allow big factories to be built in India to make the things Britain was selling. This held back Indian industry and stopped it developing.

To fight this, some people said that Indian people shouldn't buy things that weren't made in India. They should only buy things made in India.

The Hindi word meaning "from your own country" is Swadeshi so people who had these ideas became known as the Swadeshi Movement.

Gandhi told Indian women and men not to buy British goods, especially cloth. He asked them to spin their own cotton on the charka and to make khadi on handlooms.

The movement was popular. Sweetmakers wouldn't use foreign sugar, laundries wouldn't wash foreign clothes, students wouldn't use foreign paper. Because of this, small industries to make these things were started all over India.

But still there was little industry in India. There were no big factories to make steel, for example. Production was on a small scale, what we call cottage industry. Britain still wanted India to have to rely on importing things from Britain. British profits would be less if Indian people made what they needed themselves.

ACTIVITY:

1. Give each paragraph a title. Choose the titles from this list: Cottage Industry; British Goods; Indian Industry; Popularity; Indian Cloth; the Swadeshi Movement.

2. Underline in red underline parts of the story which explain how the British ruined Indian industry.

3. Underline in blue parts of the story which tell us what Indian people did as a protest.

4. Underline in green the parts of the story which tell us why it was called the Swadeshi Movement.'

Such activities can also be extended beyond texts and developed in a similar fashion with pictures and maps. For example, on an old map of a city centre, canals might be coloured in blue, tramlines in red, factories in brown and so on. In each case, the idea is to aid comprehension and to lead children towards understanding.

Another problem which children face in the enquiry process is being asked to read daunting amounts of text. There are various techniques which help overcome this. One of these is the idea of a newsroom simulation which puts children in the position of receiving news about an historic event as it comes out. A suitable example might be Julius Caesar's first visit to Britain. To carry out such work, children should be organised into groups of four or five, and the task is for these groups to report the news from a particular perspective, in this case a Roman perspective and a British perspective. They might be given a briefing sheet along the lines of:

Roman Times

It is 54 BC. You work for a newspaper called the *Roman Times*. You are proud of Rome. You are proud that Roman people go all over the world. You think Julius Caesar is a great man. You want to see his army do well. You think that British people have been helping the Gauls to fight the Romans and that they should be taught a lesson.

Activity:

'Write a report of what happened in 54 BC. You will be given some news flashes and press releases every now and then. Use them to help you write your report.'

Once they are organised in their groups newsflashes can be fed to pupils at suitable intervals. These newsflashes need not be more than a sentence or two long. For example:

Message 1: 54 BC

Gaul:

Julius Caesar says that people in Britain are helping the Gauls. He wants to stop them.

He says he will sail to Britain to teach them a lesson. He hopes it will be a rich place.

Message 2: 54 BC

Gaul:

Julius Caesar's army has set sail. He is taking 11,000 soldiers with him. Some ships can't sail because the tide is wrong. You can get pictures from the press office.

Message 3: 54 BC

Britain:

British leaders say they will be waiting for Julius Caesar when he comes. They think they can beat him.

When all the messages are received, the groups can compile the information into the newspaper article, which could, of course, be typed up using word processing or desk-top publishing software. Similarly, the messages themselves can be put on computer, using software that will enable the computer to release them automatically at suitable intervals. It is, of course, essential that children aren't misled by such work into thinking that the Romans and the Britons had computers or press rooms, but this is far outweighed by the immediacy of this technique.

The same technique can be used at Key Stages 3 and 4. Figure 7.11 shows an example of a piece of work produced about Chartist riots in Birmingham in 1839 using a similar newsroom simulation. Again, the context of history has been used not only to demonstrate historical knowledge and understanding but also to develop information technology skills at a fairly high level in the area of communication and handling information. In this case, a word processing package which allows the use of imported images and variations in fonts and font styles and size has been used. The end product, although far from perfect as a piece of history work, was something of which the group of girls involved in its production were very proud. The use of IT had helped them cope with the demands of communicating clearly and effectively.

CHARTISTS DISAGREEMENT

Today millions of chartists have gathered at Holloway Hall to put there point across. Fergus O' Conner has come to speak to the Chartists.

In his speech he pleaded and begged the people of Birmingham to use all force needed to support the Charter. Eye witnesses that were present say that he was wildly applauded with lots of enthusiasm.

The Chartist meeting have been banned unfairly.We as chartist supporters think that the behaviour of the people was acceptable and justified.We feel that the opposition were angry because we were on the verge of winning.A clan of chartist called the National Covention have come saying they will frighten parliment to submit to their demands.We would like the citizens of Birmingham to strike,the employers are concerned about this development.

Reports have shown that the local men are giving deadly threats to use home made weapons againt the police and against the the calvary.People are afraid to go out.

Rumour has it that the chartists are preparing for violence which are untrue,but as we have said previously we will use violence by all means nessary.Chartist have rejected the mayors proposals saying they are way to late and most definately continue to meet at New Street.

The Chartist have marched to the Bull Ring.Large crowds have gatherd in Bull Ring to hear Chartist leader Feargus O'Conner restated his calls for the use of force.Witnesses say that O'Conner was cheered loudly.Police have been alerted in case trouble starts.

A large crowd has again joined together to listen to another of Feargus O' Connors speechs.

The Chartist are annoyed as on of their men have been murdered.The Chartists say that the attack was uncalled for.

The Bull Ring was closed and so were the shops in the High Street.It was just a BEASTLY attack.

Thomas Atwood presented the Chartist's petition to the parliment.It was signed by over 1,280,000 people! However, MP's claimed that many of the signatures were forged.Atwood had hoped and prayed the pitition would persuade Parliment to pass the six acts of the Charter.He was very dissappointed,when,after a long debate,his proposition was thrown out.Some MP's said the Charter was worded in such a way that it was disrespectful to Parliament.

REPORTED BY :GAYLE,MELISHA,MALIEKA,NADIA and KELLY.

Figure 7.11

Within the level descriptions, progression in communication is only very partially covered. Indeed, until level 4, the notion of communication is absent as an explicit component of the descriptions:

- Level 4 – They are beginning to produce structured work, making appropriate use of dates and terms.
- Level 5 – They select and organise information to produce structured work, making appropriate use of dates and terms.
- Level 6 – They select, organise and deploy relevant information to produced structured work, making appropriate use of dates and terms.
- Level 7 – They select, organise and deploy relevant information to produce well structured narratives, descriptions and explanations, making appropriate use of dates and terms.
- Level 8 – They select, organise and deploy relevant information to produce consistently well structured narratives, descriptions and explanations, making appropriate use of dates and terms.

The major emphasis here in terms of progression is clearly the development of structure and the move towards distinct types of work: narratives, descriptions and explanations.

This progression is mirrored in the proposed new GCSE criteria for history which at Grade C require candidates to demonstrate their ability to:

'produce structured descriptions and explanations of the events, personalities and developments studied. These will show understanding of relevant causes, consequences and changes; produce structured descriptions which consider the key features and characteristics of the periods, societies and situations studied and of a variety of ideas, attitudes and beliefs held by people at the time.' (SCAA, 1994m)

To achieve Grade A, matching progression in the National Curriculum, there is a move away from description and towards producing 'developed, reasoned and well substantiated descriptions, analyses and explanations' (SCAA, 1994m).

This, of course, has not been an exhaustive survey. Materials quoted are, of necessity, merely examples. But they can be extended beyond the particular contexts mentioned here, to ensure that children are not simply 'told' history, but learn it; do not simply regurgitate others words but communicate their own understanding of the past for themselves. Planning for progression and continuity in both enquiry and communication is important if young people are to be able to achieve in history and, simultaneously, demonstrate that achievement. Despite all the criticisms, the National Curriculum for history has helped to formalise good practice and, increasingly, to ensure that children at Key Stages 1 and 2 get a thorough grounding in the skills of enquiry and communication. This is now, no longer, a matter just for Key Stages 3 and 4. Ultimately, this will ensure improvements in results and a general raising of standards in history at GCSE and beyond.

Acknowledgements

The work shown in Figure 7.3 was done using Minnie, a word processing package published by Top Class Software and Birmingham City Council Education Department Curriculum Support Service. The examples of pupils work in the chapter were done at Turves Green J. I. School, Welford J. I. School, St. Marys CofE J. I. School, Lordswood Boys School and Handsworth Wood Girls School in Birmingham.

8

Looking beyond National Curriculum history: ensuring continuity and progression after 16

James Kilmartin

In 1990 Sean Lang published a seminal study of *A level History: The Case for Change*. He argued for a radical change in the methods of teaching the subject in the sixth form, finding the menu then on offer to students limited and uninspiring (Lang, 1990). Since then there have been a number of key developments in the subject. Many of these have been syllabus driven and targeted at A level specifically. The introduction of completely new syllabi, such as the Cambridge History Project and London Syllabus E, along with major modifications made to others, such as those offered by the NEAB, have fundamentally altered the nature of A level History.

During the same period teachers of history have also witnessed and managed the introduction of the National Curriculum. In many ways this has revolutionised the teaching and learning of history in the lower school. The 1993 report by OFSTED on the implementation of the National Curriculum in history at Key Stage 3 recorded substantial progress by teachers and learners in coming to grips with attainment targets, prescribed programmes of study and the use of historical artefacts (OFSTED, 1993a). All of this, of course, has followed on from and supported the developments brought about by the more progressive GCSE syllabi introduced in the 1980s.

In certain respects Sean Lang's 'case for change' has been superceded by events. But it would be wrong to suggest that his analysis is redundant. For as in all historical processes elements of continuity abound. In many ways the changes of recent years have emphasised the yawning gap between history at A level and the preceding curriculum. Patterns of assessment, the nature of teaching and the demands made on pupils remain radically different before and after 16. Such discontinuity is damaging. This chapter will seek to focus on ways in which A level history can meet the challenge of GCSE and the National Curriculum.

The chapter will begin by identifying the major elements of discontinuity and the primary obstacles to progression in the subject. It will then go on to look at the areas of possible and necessary change. The final section will examine how far and in what ways the new or reformed syllabi live up to the challenges posed by GCSE and the National Curriculum.

One of the great difficulties to face anybody writing about A level history is the dearth of research into how the subject is delivered. In this context Sean Lang's booklet provides some of the most recent evidence about the teaching and learning of history in the sixth form. Among teachers of A level history there have been a variety of responses to the changing demands of students and syllabi. One of the most common has been to ignore them. It would appear that there are countless schools and colleges where the delivery of the subject in the sixth form has been virtually mummified. As a body of knowledge history has been embalmed with a staid mixture of chalk, talk and photocopied notes. This has been despite radical changes in the nature of the student intake and far-reaching alterations in much loved syllabi (Lang, 1990).

If tackled, many institutions would defend these practices vigorously and some indeed would have grounds for doing so. Consistently high exam results, successful entry to Oxbridge and the continuing willingness of students to register and attend would be marshalled as factors in favour of the status quo.

Of course for other schools and colleges the task of defending current practice would be more difficult. Steadily declining grades, a withering student base and a growing drop-out rate would provide evidence to any objective observer of crisis. In such institutions the new reality could not be ignored. The gap between former and recent achievement would have to be explained and explanations would have to be furnished. A 'peculiar exam paper' is one of the most popular tales of woe. But the current vogue is to blame the victim. The argument goes something like this: since the disappearance of O level the quality of the students has declined sharply. They no longer know how to write essays, partly because they no longer know how to read books. The clear implication is that GCSE (and this analysis may soon be extended to the National Curriculum) is not preparing students adequately for the demands of A level.

Such arguments should not be dismissed lightly. All of those expressing them will be professionals deeply concerned about (and occasionally dismayed by) standards. In all of these contentions there is more than an element of truth. There are some institutions where history at A level flourishes on a bed of traditional practice. Exam papers **can** be variable, inappropriate and badly targeted. There **has** been a change in the nature of the pupil intake and, as a result of this and the greater emphasis in GCSE upon sourcework, students **do** find it difficult to write essays and read extensively.

But however cogent or convincing such explanations are, the central problem remains. There is a sharp and growing discontinuity between the teaching and learning of history before and after 16. If Dearing is to be believed there will be no major changes to the National Curriculum for 5 years. Given this reality the onus is upon those who design and deliver A level to find ways of ensuring continuity and development in the 'new sixth'.

There is a further dimension to the challenge facing us. History will no longer be a foundation subject at Key Stage 4 of the National Curriculum. Subject and teachers will now have to compete for pupils and periods in an overcrowded timetable. For most history departments the opportunities and threats offered by the new context will be immediately apparent at GCSE. But it will not be long before the shock waves of change are felt at A level. So how should we react?

Firstly, teachers of history cannot afford to stick their heads in the sand. The new reality demands a new approach. The alternative is decline and disarray. It is a long way from Key Stage 3 to A level. Many potential history students will get lost along the way, seduced by the bright lights of the remaining foundation subjects, newly available social sciences and the vocational path to higher education. Of course much will depend upon how well the subject can be sustained at GCSE. The evidence suggests that it remains relatively popular as an option at this level. In 1994 a total of 227,395 candidates took the GCSE exam, a significant increase on the previous year. History is the sixth most popular subject at this level. The number was up from 215,922 in 1993. This compared with a decline in the numbers doing geography and English. It is all the more important then that A level teachers build upon this success rather than deride it.

Put simply, A level history will have to change to meet the challenge of the National Curriculum and GCSE, not the other way around. This is an opportunity rather than a problem. The teaching and learning of history prior to 16 has been revitalised in recent years. In the following pages there will be an attempt to outline the contours of necessary change, to reflect upon how far they are being followed by the current range of syllabi and, finally, to identify measures which need to be taken to sustain and nurture the subject beyond the National Curriculum.

To ensure a greater degree of continuity between the National Curriculum, GCSE and A level attention has to be paid to four main areas. These are balance within the programme of study, forms of assessment, the relationship between skills and content and, finally, the idea of history as a preparation for life.

The notion of balance between political, economic, social and cultural history was arguably one of the most ambitious concepts to arise with the National Curriculum. The extent to which it has been realised is debatable and, with less prescription following the Dearing review, will vary from institution to institution. Nevertheless the understanding of the desirability for such balance is there and pupils will have been assured of a varied diet from the past as a result. There is little in the way of a matching aspiration at A level (though see comments below on the new subject core). With some exceptions syllabi remain overwhelmingly political. Matters of culture, society and economics tend to be included, at best, in a marginal or instrumental manner.

While it would be ludicrous to deny the importance of politics in history there are other ingredients to the past. Moreover many pupils appear predisposed against the dominance of politics in history. With time and good teaching that prejudice may disappear but the point is that pupils used to a rich diet of, for example, changing life in town and countryside, women in the two world wars, cultural diversity and medicine through time, will not take kindly (perhaps not take at all) the stodge of Gladstone's four ministries and a gruelling trip through '57 varieties' of European Nationalism.

A central factor in a student's choice at A level is the assessment regime on offer. Experience suggests that, having become used to it at GCSE, many students look for a relatively high element of coursework in the subjects they choose. They may well be disappointed. It is true that many A level syllabi now contain an element of coursework (accounting usually for about 25% of the marks available) but that coursework is often restricted to one piece of extended work. One of the reasons why students choose A levels with a proportion of coursework is that, quite rationally, they wish to spread the risk. The predominant pattern in history of two terminal exams plus a personal study provides only minimal insurance. Moreover the degree of continuity with GCSE or Key Stage 4 of the National Curriculum is low. There pupils are allowed between two and seven opportunities to show their ability outside of the terminal exam.

Of course the debate over the value of coursework still rages. The quality of the contributions to it is highly variable and the motives of some of those seeking to restrict or eliminate the coursework element questionable. Teachers and students do operate within a highly political environment and it is important, therefore, that coursework is designed, delivered and completed to maintain the confidence of universities, employers and the wider public.

In this context the current mode of coursework at A level should be reviewed. The personal study or individual assignment is, at best, a brave start on the road to a satisfactory means of offering mixed ability students an opportunity to show what they can do. The theory behind it appears to be that it offers students a chance to be historians. But historians need to be trained. Even at postgraduate level students often spend their first year acquiring and cultivating the skills and knowledge necessary for them to embark upon the process of serious historical research. The selection of a topic, identification of a question, the location of sources, the analysis of evidence and the communication of historical knowledge are high level skills which many of those doing A level will simply not have, or at least not to the extent that is required.

This is not at all surprising. Neither is the fact that many students produce mediocre or even poor studies which leave them (and their teachers) with a sense of disappointment and failure. What is surprising is the high quality of work produced by some students despite the lack of preparation in research skills offered beforehand. Clearly it would be wrong to deprive high-ability students of the opportunity to produce an extended piece of writing based upon research over a period of time. But alternatives need to be offered. Shorter pieces which test specific skills and offer students the opportunity to communicate their findings in a variety of ways (orally, through drama, by the creation of a database) would enhance the potential of history as a cross curricular subject and increase the level of continuity between GCSE and A level. It would also be a recognition of the fact that not all A level history students want or need to be embryonic historians. Most employers, moreover, want people with a variety of communicative skills who can work on short term projects under pressure.

Another area of great contention in the debate over school history has been the balance between skills and content. Arguably this has been the most vacuous and staged of all the arguments surrounding the teaching and learning of the subject. Most good teachers understand the need for both skills and knowledge. One of the major spin-offs of the National Curriculum and, before that, the advent of GCSE has been the recognition that, important as they are, the narrative and the content are not the only elements which history can offer its students. The ability to analyse causation and consequence, to make use of a wide variety of evidence and to demonstrate an empathetic understanding over time and space and communicate such an analysis imaginatively and efficiently are also key weapons in the armoury of the successful pupil and potential employee. Despite overload, Key Stage 3 and GCSE provide a framework for the development of both knowledge and skills.

Many would argue that, until recently, A level syllabi have been too heavily laden. Indeed some have gone as far as to refer to the 'tyranny of content'. One does not need to adopt such a dramatic turn of phrase to agree with the sentiment behind it. How many students (and teachers!) have experienced the panic of whole centuries in the night before their terminal exam. While extensive knowledge of the past is admirable, even entertaining, the danger is that such an unhealthy concern with what happened will divert teachers and students away from other questions and themes which need to be considered – such as those discussed earlier in this book.

Finally, this section must consider how effectively A level continues the preparation of students for life beyond subject and school. Within programmes of study in the National Curriculum teachers have been obliged to identify cross-curricular links and themes as appropriate. The relevance of history to other subjects in the National Curriculum (notably religious education, geography and English) is clear, as is its potential for contributing to citizenship, economic understanding and environmental awareness.

Once again A level appears disappointing by comparison, isolated in a disciplinary and academic ghetto. Partly because of the 'need to get on', the desire to plough through heavily laden syllabi, there are relatively few opportunities to take a wider view and hardly any tangible rewards for doing so.

Of course it is only the examination boards and assessment authorities who can change this situation. Necessarily and rationally teachers and students will only alter their approach if there is reason for doing so. Before we go on to examine the extent to which the masters of the assessment game have responded to the challenge of GCSE and the National Curriculum as a whole it is worth refocusing on the four areas of suggested change.

Firstly there must be an attempt to offer students a more varied and balanced programme of study, chiefly through the provision of more social, cultural and economic options. Secondly the nature and extent of coursework should be reviewed with an eye towards a more realistic and relevant format which does not assume that all A level students have an inherent grasp of sophisticated research techniques. The dominance of the one-off piece of extended writing needs to be questioned and other menus (more pieces targeted at the development of specific skills) offered. Thirdly content led syllabi need to be modified to facilitate an increasing appreciation of historiographical issues and the cultivation of the wide range of skills which the subject can offer. Finally history at A level should be enabled to escape the disciplinary strait-jacket it currently occupies and promote itself as a subject rich in cross-curricular and interdisciplinary potential. Only by implementing such a programme will we be able to ensure greater continuity with GCSE and the National Curriculum and provide our students with the best opportunity to develop and enhance their skills, knowledge and understanding.

Now is the time to make these changes. Certainly there is no lack of encouragement from the top. The recently published A/AS subject core for history began with an explicit commitment to ensure progression from the National Curriculum and GCSE. The language of the document as a whole is intriguing: National Curriculum speak abounds! The criteria for the selection of content includes the desire for 'a range of historical perspectives...political, social, economic, cultural, technological, intellectual and religious'. There is a clear determination that A level syllabi should follow the lead given in the lower school. The general commitment to examining the diversity of society is followed by a specific instruction to look at the experiences of both men and women. British history is to be just that: the Scots, the Welsh and the Irish should not simply be bit players in an English drama. In the section on knowledge and understanding of content there is a clear injunction to enable candidates not only to 'demonstrate knowledge' but also to show 'their understanding of methodological concepts such as cause, change and development'. The proposals are notably less adventurous when it comes to how the subject should be assessed but that is perhaps understandable given the political currency of coursework (SCAA, 1994k).

The core criteria is, at best, a general guideline for examination boards. It will be some years before we can judge how effectively they have been realised. So how well do current syllabi meet the challenge of GCSE and the National Curriculum? The first point to make is that since Sean Lang's survey of A level history was published in 1990 there have been a number of new syllabi which have either completed their pilot stage, such as the Cambridge History Project, become newly available or, sadly, been abandoned. We are dealing with a fluid rather than a static situation.

The first of the modern A level syllabi in history to become available was AEB's 673. This was first examined in 1977. For this syllabus students do three papers. Paper one is a period study while paper two is an examination of theory and evidence in history. Both are assessed by terminal examination only. Paper three is a personal study worth 25% of the marks. This syllabus is well established and successful. The fact that it incorporates source and coursework gives it a clear claim to continuity with GCSE and, beyond that, the National Curriculum.

Much, however, depends upon how the syllabus is delivered. The obvious temptation is to teach to the papers, dividing the time available between the period study (worth 50% of the marks) and the rest. The problem with such an approach is that, in sharp contrast to the situation at Key Stage 3, sources and content can end up being taught independently of each other, leaving students with a rather peculiar sense of how historians work.

When AEB introduced its new syllabus it was considered to be something of a revolution. Nearly 20 years on it still provides a framework for innovation and good practice. There is a good choice of content papers available to teachers and students and at least one of these, aspects of world history since 1945, encourages those following it to adopt a non-Eurocentric approach to a period of time which has seen the emergence of new nations and a polarisation of the developed and the developing worlds.

The most innovatory aspect of 673, at conception, was the personal study. A mini-dissertation based upon the student's own researches, it is potentially an exciting opportunity for a candidate to identify an area of interest and get close to the experience of actually making history. That history can include studies of those normally relegated to the footnotes of the recorded past and can incorporate social, cultural and economic themes as well as the more familiar political issues. Over the years some superb pieces of work have emerged.

But there are problems with this aspect of the syllabus. The greatest of these is time. In many ways the personal study was simply bolted on to a pre-existing syllabus (630). There were now three papers instead of two! Of course in most schools and colleges it has been quite impossible to gain a proportionate, or even a token, increase in the timetable allocation for history. As a result the personal study – particularly if it is not related to the period paper – has had to be completed and managed on the margins. Given that it is probably the most challenging piece of work a history student will undertake before their final year at university this is a strange state of affairs. But it is probably the case in many institutions.

The nature of the personal study (in this and other syllabi) as coursework should also be a matter of concern. For while it does provide an element of continuity with GCSE (in terms of marks being awarded outside of the terminal exam) it is only an element. For the personal study is a creature on its own, quite different from the pattern of coursework which students will have experienced before. It provides students with one big bite at the assessment apple outside of the exam hall. Given that many students experience problems (quite predictable and understandable) with such an extensive piece of work this is not a wholly reassuring, or perhaps an entirely fair and pedagogically wise, scenario.

One of the most innovative of all the new syllabi is the Cambridge History Project (People, Power and Politics). This has completed its pilot stage and is now a fully operational syllabus. At inception the differences between it and the traditional approach to history were startling. The most novel aspect of the CHP was the assessment regime. Originally students were assessed on the basis of six domains. Each domain was directed at a skill or concept and within these domains three levels of achievement were possible. One-third of the marks were available for coursework, the remainder had to be earned in the final exam. During the pilot stage one piece of coursework had to be an oral exercise.

Following the pilot (which was distinguished by a high level of consultation and the commitment of an extraordinarily accessible chief examiner, Bob Ellis) a number of changes were introduced. The number of domains has been reduced to three and so has the number of coursework exercises. The oral coursework is now optional.

The great value of the Cambridge History Project for teachers of history is that it forces them to think about how and why the subject is taught. The breakdown of the discipline into its component skills and concepts, along with the need to decode the overly technical language used, has challenged all of those involved to rethink their approach.

Perhaps the most welcome feature of the CHP is the emphasis upon skills and concepts as well as content. Students spend half of their time on a depth study (the English Revolution c.1640–1660) and half on the development study where the emphasis is upon a thematic approach to a thousand years of history.

How far, then, can the CHP be said to build on the experience and achievement of pupils at GCSE and in the National Curriculum? The first point to make is that the CHP has left the personal study model of coursework behind. Students get three bites at the cherry, at various points in the two-year cycle. They do exercises which test specific and differentiated competences. This pattern of assessment has a good deal more in common with the National Curriculum and GCSE than anything which has gone before.

One feature of CHP which will become increasingly useful in relation to the National Curriculum is the development study. Dealing with political change over time, this should allow students to revisit, in more analytical garb, periods and places familiar to them from Years 7 to 9 and, possibly, GCSE. For at present the development study remains problematical for teachers and students alike. Although this side of the CHP is a genuine attempt to get away from the 'tyranny of content' it does, ironically, presume a lot of knowledge and understanding. There must be genuine concern too that students are presented with a somewhat idiosyncratic view of the past based on pre-selected sources. It is certainly the part of the course with which most students feel uncomfortable.

The depth study is well thought out. Students begin with an overview and move on to examine events, issues and themes within a modular framework. There are plenty of opportunities to examine historiographical debates and to question the nature of the evidence available. While much of the study is concerned with events at Westminster the perspectives and experience of the common people, men and women is looked at seriously and care has been taken to choose a range of exciting and varied sources. Overall students appear to find this the most satisfying part of their work, building upon skills and concepts accumulated in years 7 to 11.

Like the development study the depth study offers a pre-selection of primary and secondary evidence. Students rarely get the opportunity to look at complete sources, often having to make do with short extracts. This appears to be at odds with good practice from Key Stages 1 to 3 where pupils should be learning how to select appropriate sources themselves. Those following the syllabus can, of course, read outside and beyond the prescribed material but there will surely be a tendency for most pupils to take what they get and to avoid the challenge of whole books and complete documents. The depth study is also rather Anglo-centric, although it is true that attention is paid to the idea of a British rather than an English revolution and candidates get the opportunity, in the last module of the study, to set the events of the mid-seventeenth century in a wider European context. This is, however, precisely the point in the two-year cycle where many teachers are looking for short cuts and the temptation must surely be for many to deliver this module in a truncated manner where clear lines of comparison are spoon fed to students eager for the security of lecture style notes.

The third major syllabus to be considered is London Syllabus E. Following the rather sad demise of ETHOS this has become a popular choice for innovative departments. The great attraction of Syllabus E is that it allows teachers to design a programme of coursework themselves, making use of resources and the expertise of staff. This is a challenging task and has to be completed within a set of guidelines which emphasise the need to provide students with contrast over time, space and in the nature of the historical approach. Given that most of the examined papers look at political events the onus is, therefore, upon teachers to focus upon social, economic and cultural issues. The torch has been passed.

Syllabus E has a relatively high level of continuous assessment. Students do four pieces of coursework, worth up to 30% of total marks, and one individual assignment which can earn up to 20% of the marks available. Students also do two exam papers which, broadly speaking, can be described as a period and a depth study.

This is an objective-led syllabus and, to that extent, it has a strong claim to continuity with GCSE. The students are assessed in a variety of ways (one piece of coursework has to be carried out under controlled circumstances and only two of the four pieces have to be in written form) and the individual assignment can be done in a collaborative manner.

The same basic idea lies behind the individual assignment as inspired the personal study in AEB 673. It is an opportunity for students to choose an area of particular interest and focus upon it in a detailed way. Nevertheless there are substantial differences. Firstly students can determine part of the assessment regime themselves. One half of the marks are awarded for one objective, but pupils can then determine how the remaining 50% should relate to the objectives. In AEB 673 the assessment regime (laid out in an awesome grid) is fixed. The Syllabus E approach allows students who want to do a particular kind of study (one, for example, which concentrates on historiographical issues rather than the role of an individual in history) to design an appropriate test for their work.

The exams too allow students to build on their experience at GCSE. Although still a component of each paper there is less emphasis upon the traditional essay and more upon the use and evaluation of sources and the analysis of historiographical issues.

Syllabus E provides a very clear degree of continuity with GCSE. A rather different approach has been adopted by the NEAB in their revised alternatives. They too have tried to challenge the tyranny of content. They have done this by providing specific guidance on the content to be examined and by identifying key questions for each of the periods studied. An element of coursework is available, although in this case the model adopted has been that of the personal study worth 25% of the marks.

NEAB provides a range of new style syllabi, some of which provide students with an exciting opportunity to look at history from a variety of perspectives. The A level in modern Irish history, for example, begins by looking at the history of the Irish in Britain and goes on to look at the relationship between literature, nationalism and the Irish identity. This is a highly enjoyable and coherent syllabus to teach, one which facilitates a search for appropriate sources and a rigorous examination of evidence in context.

There are, of course, more traditional syllabi on offer, at least in terms of the content covered. For many teachers and students the transition from the old style to a new style approach has been problematic. This year's report by the examiners on the revised alternatives makes fascinating reading and provides a useful focus for a conclusion. In the report on alternative NM (Britain 1783–1906) it is made clear that despite the radical changes to the syllabus there is clear evidence that many students are being fed exactly the same diet as their predecessors! Specifically it is noted that although the syllabus now begins in 1783 rather than 1815 (for well considered historical and pedagogical reasons) it is quite apparent that many teachers commence their review of the period in 1815 – as they have done for years! The report also reveals that the NEAB received letters of complaint from some teachers about the exam paper in general, and the absence of a question on Lord Liverpool's government in particular. Presumably the inclusion of a question on Catholic Emancipation was seen as a poor substitute for the hardy annual on Liberal Tories. Old habits (and old debates) die hard! (NEAB, 1994).

The report reveals the extent of the challenge now facing those involved in A level history. There have been genuine, varied, and often successful attempts to respond to the brave new world opened up by GCSE and the National Curriculum. Much of the revolution in the teaching of history to the over sixteens has been engineered from the top down. Syllabi and subject criteria have changed, although patterns of assessment and the balance between skills and content remain problematic and limiting in many syllabi. But at least a process has begun. It is now the time for that process to be carried forward into the classroom.

Further reading

The following texts provide further valuable information

Fisher, T. (1990) *'A' Level History: More Questions Than Answers.* Teaching History no 62.

Fullan, M. (1993) *Change Forces, Probing the Depths of Educational Reform.* London: The Falmer Press.

Kelly, A. (1990) *The National Curriculum, A Critical Review.* London: Paul Chapman.

OFSTED (1993) *GCE Advanced Supplementary and Advanced Level Examinations.* London: HMSO.

Taylor, L. (1994) *Responses to the Dearing Report: History Post-16.* Teaching History no 75.

White, C. (1994) 'Defence of the realms', *Times Educational Supplement,* **8 April.**

Bibliography

Adams, C. (1981) 'Off the record', *Teaching History*, **36**, 3–6.

Adams, R. (1991) *Medieval Realms*. Ormskirk: Causeway.

Adler, S. *et al.* (undated, c.1993) *Putting Women into the History Curriculum, Women in Tudor and Stuart Times*, Islington Education Service and Islington Women's Equality Unit.

Alexander, R. (1994) '"What Primary Curriculum?" Dearing and Beyond', *Education,* **3 (13)**, 24–35.

Allison, R. and Brown, C. (1990) *Medieval Realms*. Dunstable: Folens.

Anderson, B. (1983) *Imagined Communities, Reflections on the Origins and Spread of Nationalism*. London: Verso.

Appleby, J., Hunt, L. and Jacob, M. (1994) *Telling the Truth about History*. New York: W.W.Norton.

Ashby, R. and Lee, P. (1987) 'Children's concepts of empathy and understanding in history' in Portal, C. (ed.) *The History Curriculum for Teachers*. Lewes: The Falmer Press, pp.62–88.

Aylett, J.F. (1991) *Medieval Realms 1066–1500*. London: Hodder & Stoughton.

Bage, G (1993) 'History at Key Stage 1 and Key Stage 2: questions of teaching, planning, assessment and progression', *The Curriculum Journal,* **4 (2)**, 269–82.

Baldwin, G. (1994) 'A Dearing Opportunity: History Teaching and Moral Education', *Teaching History*, **76**, 29–32.

Bentham (1994) 'Fireworks over plot to ditch Guy Fawkes', *Daily Express,* 5 May.

Blackburne, L. (1994) 'Group battles endemic racism', *Times Educational Supplement,* 15 July.

Blatchford, R. and Howard, R. (1993) *Primary–Secondary Continuity into Practice*, Harlow: Longman.

De Bono, E. (1994) 'When is a box not a box? When it's a straitjacket', *Guardian*, 3 August, **27**.

Booth, M. (1987) 'Ages and concepts: A Critique of the Piagetan Approach to History Teaching', in Portal, C. (ed.) *The History Curriculum for Teachers*. Lewes: The Falmer Press, pp.22–38.

Bourdillon, H. (1994) 'On the record: the importance of gender in the teaching history', in Bourdillon, H. (ed.) *Teaching History*. London: Routledge, pp.62–75.

Brace, G. (1994) 'The "F–Plan" Approach to National Curriculum History'. *Welsh Historian*, **21**, 3–7.

Briggs, A. (1990) in Gardiner, J. (ed.) *The History Debate*, London: Collins & Brown, pp.61–7.

Broomfield, S. (1992) *Welsh National Curriculum History: Wales in the Medieval World*. Brighton: Spartacus.

Bruner, J.S. (1960) *The Process of Education*. Cambridge, Ma.: Harvard University Press.

Collins, J. and Taylor, C. (1992) 'Differentiation at Key Stage 3 – Mathematics and History', *All-In Success,* **4 (3)**, 8–11.

Cannadine, D. (1987) 'British History: Past, Present and Future', *Past and Present*, **116**, 169–91.

Carr, E.H. (1964) *What is History?*, Harmondsworth: Penguin.

Castles, S. (1993) 'Migration and minorities in Europe', in Wrench, J. and Solomos, J. (eds.) *Racism and Migration in Western Europe*. Oxford: Berg.

CCW (1993) *Progression and Differentiation in History at Key Stage 3*. Cardiff: Curriculum

Council for Wales.

Chitty, C. (1988) 'Two Models of a National Curriculum: origins and interpretation', in Lawton, D. and Chitty, C. (eds.) *The National Curriculum*. London: Kogan Page, pp.34–64.

Collicot, S. (1993) 'A Way of Looking at History: Local – National – World Links' *Teaching History*, **72**, 18–23.

Colwill, I. (1992) 'A Study of National Curriculum Assessment', *Welsh Historian*, **18**, 3–5.

Connelly, F. (1994) 'What is the Future for National Curriculum History?', *Teaching History*, **74**, 23–26.

Cooper, H. (1992) *The Teaching of History*, London: David Fulton.

Cooper, H. (1994) 'Children's learning, Key Stage 2: Recent Findings', in John, P. and Lucas, P. (eds) *Partnership and Progress*, Sheffield: SCHTE in the UK in association with The Division of Education: University of Sheffield, 102–15.

Cowie, L. (1970) *The Pilgrim Fathers*. Hove: Wayland.

Cross, J., Hodkinson, S., Jackson, P., McFarlane, C., and Sprackling, A. (1994) *Long Ago and Far Away: Activities for Using Stories for History and Geography at Key Stage 1*. Birmingham: Development Education Centre.

Culpin, C. (1994) 'Making Progress in History', in Bourdillon, H. (ed.) *Teaching History*. London: Routledge, pp.126–52.

Curtis, S. and Bardwell, S. (1994) 'Access to History', in Bourdillon, H. (ed.) *Teaching History*. London: Routledge, pp.169–88.

Dawson, I. and Watson, P. (1991) *Medieval Realms*. Oxford: Oxford University Press.

Deans, J. (1994) 'Lessons on Guy Fawkes could soon be history', *Daily Mail*, **28 February**.

Dearing, R. (1994) *The National Curriculum and its Assessment.* London: SCAA.

DES (1983) *Curriculum 11–16. Towards a Statement of Entitlement.* London: HMSO.

DES (1985) *History in the Primary and Secondary Years. An HMI View.* London: HMSO.

DES (1987) *The National Curriculum 5–16. A Consultation Document.* London: DES.

DES (1988) *History from 5–16. Curriculum Matters 11.* London: HMSO.

DES (1989) *From Policy to Practice.* London: HMSO.

DES (1990a) *National Curriculum History Working Group: Final Report.* London: HMSO.

DES (1990b) *History for Ages 5–16.* London: HMSO.

DES (1991) *History in the National Curriculum (England).* London: HMSO.

DFE (1995) *The History Order.* London: DFE.

Dickinson, A.K. and Lee, P.J. (1984) 'Making Sense of History', in Dickinson, A.K., Lee, P.J. and Rogers, P.J. (eds) *Learning History*. London: Heinemann, pp.117–53.

Dickinson, A. (1991) 'Assessing, Recording and Reporting Children's Achievements: from Changes to Genuine Gains', in Aldrich, R. (ed.) *History in the National Curriculum*. London: Kogan Page, pp.66–93.

Dickinson, A. and Lee, P. (1994) 'Investigating Progression in Children's Ideas about History: the CHATA project', in John, P. and Lucas, P. (eds) *Partnership and Progress*, Sheffield: SCHTE in the UK in association with The Division of Education: University of Sheffield, pp.78–101.

Evans, N. (1988) 'Debate, British History, Past, Present and Future', *Past and Present*, **119 (111)** 194–203.

Farmer, A. (1991) *Invaders and Settlers*. London: Guinn.

Fentress, J. and Wickham, C. (1992) *Social Memory*. Oxford: Blackwell.

Fiehn, T. and Shephard, C. (1993) *History into Practice*. London: Longman.

Fines, J. (1994) 'Progression – A Seminar Report', *Teaching History*, **75**, 27–8.

Fines, J. and Nichol, J. (1994) *ETHOS Doing History 16–19: A Case Study in Curriculum Innovation and Change*. London: Historical Association with assistance from the Nuffield Foundation.

Fisher, P. and Williams, N. (1989) *Past into Present 3. 1700 – The Present Day*. London: Collins.

Furedi, F. (1992) *Mythical Past and Elusive Future*. London: Pluto Press.

Garvey, B. and Krug, M. (1977) *Models of History Teaching in the Secondary School*. Oxford: Oxford University Press.

Gosden, P. and Sylvester, D. (1968) *History for the Average Child*. Oxford: Basil Blackwell.

Grosvenor, I. (1994) *Education, History and the Making of Racialised Identities in Post-1945 Britain*, unpublished PhD, University of Birmingham.

Grosvenor, I. and Watts, R. (1993) 'The Implementation of the National Curriculum in History', *Forum*, **35 (2)**, 48–50.

Ha, W. H. and Hallward, C.L.J. (1970) *A Pictorial World History: Book 2*. Cheshire: Longman.

Ha, W. H. and Hallward, C.L.J. (1980) *A Pictorial World History: Book 2*. Cheshire Harlow: Longman.

Harper, P. (1993) 'Using the Attainment Targets in Key Stage 2: AT2, "Interpretations of History"', *Teaching History*, **72**, 11–13.

Haydn, T.A. (1993) 'The chemistry of history lessons, teacher autonomy and the reform of National Curriculum History', *Welsh Historian*, **20**, 7–10.

Haydn, T.A. (1994) 'History and Employment: a Forgotten Agenda', *International Society for History Didactics Communications*, **15 (1)**, 48–56.

Hennessy, P. (1994) 'Patten gives the trendies a lesson on our history', *Daily Express*, **19 March**

H.E.Q.C. (Higher Education Quality Council) (1994) *Choosing to Change. Extending Access, Choice and Mobility in Higher Education*. London: HEQC.

Hill, D. (1994) 'Teacher Education and Training: a critique', *Forum* **36 (3)**, 74–76.

HMI (1989) *Curriculum Continuity at 11 Plus*. London: DES.

Historical Association (1991) *Conference papers Implementing the National Curriculum*. London: Historical Association.

Historical Association (1992) *Conference papers Sharing Good Practice*. London: Historical Association.

Holmes, B. (1993) 'Establishing Level-related Criteria for History', *Discoveries*, **2**, 3–8.

Hoodless, P. (1994) 'Language Use and Problem Solving in Primary History', *Teaching History*, **76**, 19–22.

Isaac, R. (June, 1994) 'Critical History?', *Teaching History*, **76**, 17–18.

Jenkins, K. (1991) *Re-thinking History*. London: Routledge.

Joseph, K. (1984) 'Why Teach History in School', *The Historian*, Spring, pp.10–12.

Kaye, H.J. (1992) *The Education of Desire. Marxists and the Writing of History*. London: Routledge.

Kearney, H. (1989) *The British Isles: A History of Four Nations*. Cambridge: Cambridge University Press.

Kearney, H. (1994) 'Four Nations or One?' in Bourdillon, H. (ed.) *Teaching History*. London: Routledge, pp.49–52.

Kelly, A. (1992) 'The Unity of Historical Activity The Attainment Targets Re–appraised'. *Welsh Historian*, **18**, 6–9.

Knight, P. (1989) 'A Study of Children's Understanding of People in the Past', *Educational Review*, **41 (3)**.

Lang, S. (1990) *A Level history: The Case for Change*. London: the Historical Association.

Lee, P.J. (1984) 'Why learn history?', in Dickinson, A.K., Lee, P.J. and Rogers P.J. (eds) *Learning History*. London: Heinemann, pp.1–19.

Lee, P. (1991) 'Historical Knowledge and the National Curriculum' in Aldrich, R. (ed.) *History in the National Curriculum*. London: Kogan Page, pp.39–65.

Lomas, T. (1993) *Teaching and Assessing Historical Understanding*. London: Historical Association.

McAleavy, T. (1991) *Medieval Britian: Conquest, Power and People* Cambridge: Cambridge University Press.

McAleavy, T. (July, 1993) 'Using the Attainment Targets in Key Stage 3: AT2, "Interpretations of History"'. *Teaching History*, **72**, 14–17.

McAleavy, T. (1994) 'Meeting pupils' learning needs; differentiation and progression in the teaching of history' in Bourdillon, H. (ed.) *Teaching History*, London: Routledge, pp.153–68.

McGovern, C. (1994) *The SCAA Review of National Curriculum History: A Minority Report*. York: Campaign for Real Education.

Mason, J. (1991a) *The Anglo–Saxons Resource Book*. Harlow: Longman.

Mason, J. (1991b) *A Sense of History: The Vikings Resource Book*. Harlow: Longman.

Mason, J. (1991c) *A Sense of History: Medieval Realms*. Harlow: Longman.

MEG (1991a) *British Social & Economic History. Optional Topics, Paper 2*. Cambridge: MEG.

MEG (1991b) *Examiners' Report: British Social & Economic History*. Cambridge: MEG.

Miles, R. (1982) *Racism and Migrant Labour*. London: Routledge.

Miles, R. (1988) *The Woman's History of the World*. London: Michael Joseph.

Miles, R.(1993) 'The Articulation of Racism and Nationalism', in Wrench, J. and Solomos, J. (eds) *Racism and Migration in Western Europe*. Oxford: Berg.

Moore, A. (1993) 'Strategies for making History Accessible to Children with Special Educational Needs', *Discoveries*, **3**, 8–13.

Myres, K. (ed.) (1992) *Genderwatch after the Education Reform Act*. Oxford: Oxford University Press.

NCC (1990a) *Guidance Document on the Whole Curriculum*. York: National Curriculum Council.

NCC (1990b) *Curriculum Guidance on Education for Citizenship*. York: National Curriculum Council.

NCC (1991a) *History Non–Statutory Guidance*. York: National Curriculum Council.

NCC (1991b) *Implementing National Curriculum History*. York: National Curriculum Council.

NCC (1991c) *Newsletter*. York: National Curriculum Council.

NCC (1993a) *Teaching History at Key Stage 1*. York: National Curriculum Council.

NCC (1993b) *Teaching History at Key Stage 2*. York: National Curriculum Council.

NCC (1993c) *Teaching History at Key Stage 3*. York: National Curriculum Council.

New Internationalist (1993) **247**.

Nichol, J. (1979) *The Vikings*. Oxford: Basil Blackwell.

Nichol, J. (1991) *Thinking History: Medieval Realms*. Oxford: Basil Blackwell.

OFSTED (1992) *History Key Stages 1, 2 & 3. First Year*, London: HMSO.

OFSTED (1993a) *History Key Stages 1, 2 & 3, Second Year*. London: HMSO.

OFSTED (1993b) *Handbook for the Inspection of Schools*. London: HMSO.

OFSTED (1994) *Spiritual, Moral, Social and Cultural Development. An OFSTED Discussion Paper*. London: HMSO.

Osler, A. (1994) 'Still Hidden from History? The representation of women in recently published textbooks', *Oxford Review of Education*, **20 (2)**, 219–34.

Page, P. and Newman, H. (1985) *They Came to Britain: The History of a Multicultural Nation*. London: Edward Arnold.

Phillips, R. (1993) 'Change and Continuity: some Reflections on the first Year's Implementation of Key Stage 3 History in the National Curriculum', *Teaching History*,**70**, 9–12.

Purkis, S. (1991) *Invaders and Settlers: Teacher's Handbook*. Harlow: Longman.

Purkis, S. (1992) *A Sense of History. Key Stage 2. Britain since 1930*. Harlow: Longman.

Richards, C. (1994) 'Four Ways Forward for Specialists', *Times Educational Supplement,* **6 May,** 9.

Roberts, M. (1994) 'Changing the course of history', *Times Educational Supplement*, **24 June**, 21.

Robson, G. (1991) 'Bebba and her Sisters', *Teaching History*, **64**, 22–5.

Robson, W. (1991) *Access to History: Medieval Realms*. Oxford: Oxford University Press.

Rogers P. (1984) 'Why learn history?', in Dickinson, A., Lee, P.J. and Rogers, P. J. (eds) *Learning History*. London: Heinemann, pp.20–38.

Rogers P. (1987) 'History – The Past as a Frame of Reference', in Portal, C. (ed.) *The History Curriculum for Teachers*. Lewes: The Falmer Press, pp.3–21.

Runnymede Trust (1992) *Equality Assurance in the School Curriculum: Race Equality and Cultural Diversity*. London: Runnymede Trust.

Sansom, C. (1987) 'Concepts, Skills and Content: A Developmental Approach to the History Syllabus', in Portal, C. (ed.) *The History Curriculum for Teachers*. Lewes: The Falmer Press.

SCAA (1994a) *The History Attainment Targets*. London: SCAA.

SCAA (1994b) *History Draft Proposals.* London: HMSO.

SCAA (1994c) *History Update.* London: SCAA.

SCAA (1994d) *Consultation on the National Curriculum.* London: SCAA.

SCAA (1994e) *National Curriculum History Response Form.* London: SCAA.

SCAA (1994f) *National Curriculum Consultation Questionnaire for History. Key Stages 1 and 2.* London: SCAA.

SCAA (1994g) *National Curriculum Consultation Questionnnaire for History. Key Stage 3.* London: SCAA.

SCAA (1994h) *National Curriculum Consultation Baseline.* London: SCAA.

SCAA (1994i) *National Curriculum Consultation History.* London: SCAA.

SCAA (1994j) *A Level Draft Criteria.* London: SCAA.

SCAA (1994k) *A/AS Subject Core for History.* London: SCAA.

SCAA (1994l) *Occasional Papers in History 1.* London: SCAA.

SCAA (1994m) *Draft GCSE Criteria for History.* London: SCAA.

Schools Council (1976) *History 13–16.* Edinburgh: Holmes McDougall.

Scott, B. (1994) 'A Post–Dearing Look at Hi.2: Interpretations of History', *Teaching History*, **75**, 20–6.

SEAC (1993) *History Standard Assessment Tasks: Key Stage 1.* London: NFER – Nelson Publishing Company.

Shemilt, D. (1980) *History 13–16 Evaluation Study Schools Council History 13–16 Project.* Edinburgh: Holmes McDougall.

Shemilt, D. (1987) 'Adolescent ideas about evidence and methodology in history', in Portal, C. (ed.) *The History Curriculum for Teachers.* Lewes: The Falmer Press, pp.39–61.

Shephard, C., Corbishley, M., Large, A. and Tames, R. (1991) *Contrasts and Connections*; London: John Murray.

Shephard, C., Hinton, C., Hite, J. and Lomas, T. (1992) *Societies in Change.* London: John Murray.

Shephard, C. (1993) 'Making sense of the attainment targets', *Discoveries*, **2**, 11.

Shephard, C. (1994) 'Differentiation and progression', *Discoveries*, **4**, 12–17.

Simon, B. (1988) *Bending the Rules. The 'Baker Reform' of Education.* London: Lawrence and Wishart.

Slater, J. (1992) 'Where are we now? Key issues in history teacher education', in Lucas, P. and Watts, R., (eds) *Meeting the Challenge.* Sheffield: Standing Conference of History Teacher Educators in the United Kingdom in association with the University of Sheffield Division of Education

Tate, N. (1994) 'Target Vision', *Times Educational Supplement*, **2 December**, 19.

Visram, R. (1994) 'British history: whose history? Black perspectives on British history', in Bourdillon, H., (ed.) *Teaching History.* London: Routledge, pp.53–61.

Warren, P. (1992) 'Interpretations of Attainment Target 2', *Discoveries*, **1**, 6–11.

Watts, R. (1992) 'History' in Ribbins, P. (ed.) *Delivering the National Curriculum.* London: Routledge, 137–56.

Watts, R. (1993) 'Implementing the National Curriculum, Term 1', *Teaching History*, **70**, 13–17.

White, C. (1992) *Strategies for the Assessment and Teaching of History.* York: Longman.

White, C. (1993) 'What is progression in History?', *Discoveries*, **3**, 3–7.

Whitlock, A. (1994) *The Leonardo Effect.* Derby: J.M. Tatler & Son.

Index